Developing Mathematical Ideas

Geometry

Measuring Space in One, Two, and Three Dimensions

Casebook

A collaborative project by the staff and
participants of Teaching to the Big Ideas

Principal Investigators

Deborah Schifter

Virginia Bastable

Susan Jo Russell

with
Kristine Reed Woleck

DALE SEYMOUR PUBLICATIONS

Pearson Learning Group

 National Science Foundation   ExxonMobil

This work was supported by the National Science Foundation under Grant Nos. ESI-9254393 and ESI-9731064. Any opinions, findings, conclusions, or recommendations expressed here are those of the authors and do not necessarily reflect the views of the National Science Foundation.

Additional support was provided by a grant from the ExxonMobil Foundation.

The following images are from *Investigations in Number, Data, and Space* (Glenview, IL: Scott Foresman, 1998), reprinted by permission of Pearson Education, Inc.: the set of seven lettered rectangles in case 4 (pp. 22-29), from J. Akers, M. Battista, A. Goodrow, D. Clements, and J. Sarama, *Shapes, Halves, and Symmetry*, a grade 2 unit; the eight "Quick Image" cube figures in case 10 (pp. 53-58), from M. Battista and D. Clements, *Seeing Solids and Silhouettes*, a grade 4 unit; the two "crazy cake" shapes in case 11 (pp. 59-61), from C. Tierney, M. Ogonowski, A. Rubin, and S. J. Russell, *Different Shapes, Equal Pieces*, a grade 4 unit; the box net in case 28 (p. 158), from M. Battista and M. Berle-Carman, *Containers and Cubes*, a grade 5 unit.

Art & Design: Jim O'Shea, Elizabeth Nemeth
Editorial: Beverly Cory, Doris Hirschhorn
Manufacturing: Mark Cirillo, Sonia Pap
Marketing: Margo Hanson
Production: Karen Edmonds, Jennifer Murphy
Publishing Operations: Carolyn Coyle

ISBN 0-7690-2787-3
Printed in the United States of America
1 2 3 4 5 6 7 8 9 10 ML 05 04 03 02 01

Dale Seymour Publications
Pearson Learning Group

This Book Is Printed on Recycled Paper

1-800-321-3106
www.pearsonlearning.com

Teaching to the Big Ideas

Developing Mathematical Ideas (DMI) was developed as a collaborative project by the staff and participants of Teaching to the Big Ideas, an NSF Teacher Enhancement Project.

PROJECT DIRECTORS   Deborah Schifter (EDC), Virginia Bastable (SummerMath for Teachers), and Susan Jo Russell (TERC)

STAFF   Jill Bodner Lester (SummerMath for Teachers), Kristine Reed Woleck (Wilton Public Schools, CT)

PARTICIPANTS   Marie Appleby, Allan Arnaboldi, Lisa Bailly, Audrey Barzey, Katie Bloomfield, Nancy Buell, Rose Christiansen, Rebeka Eston, Kimberly Formisano, Connie Henry, Nancy Horowitz, Debbie Jacque, Liliana Klass, Beth Monopoli, Deborah Morrissey, Amy Morse, Deborah Carey O'Brien, Karin Olson, Anne Marie O'Reilly, Janet Pananos, Margie Riddle, Bette Ann Rodzwell, Jan Rook, Karen Schweitzer, Malia Scott, Lisa Seyferth, Margie Singer, Susan Bush Smith, Diane Stafford, Michele Subocz, Liz Sweeney, Pam Szczesny, Jan Szymaszek, Nora Toney, Polly Wagner, and Carol Walker, representing the public schools of Amherst, Boston, Brookline, Lexington, Lincoln, Newton, Northampton, Pelham, Shutesbury, South Hadley, Southampton, Springfield, and Williamsburg, Massachusetts; the Atrium School in Watertown, Massachusetts; the Park School in Brookline, Massachusetts; and the Smith College Campus School in Northampton, Massachusetts

VIDEO DEVELOPMENT   David Smith (TERC)

CONSULTANTS   Mike Battista (Kent State University), Herb Clemens (University of Utah), Doug Clements (State University of New York at Buffalo), Cliff Konold (University of Massachusetts at Amherst), Rich Lehrer (University of Wisconsin), Gary Martin (Auburn University), Michael Mitchelmore (Macquarie University, Australia), Steve Monk (University of Washington), and Judy Roitman (University of Kansas)

FIELD TEST SITES   Albuquerque Public Schools (New Mexico), Bellevue School District (Washington), Boston Public Schools (Massachusetts), Clark County School District (Nevada), Holyoke Public Schools (Massachusetts), Lake Washington School District (Washington), Moreno Valley School District (California)

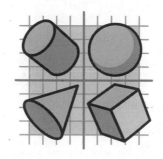

C O N T E N T S

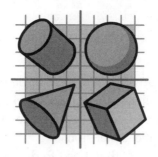

Introduction

Teachers have always included lessons on measurement in their work. In elementary schools, students may learn how to pace off a length, use a ruler, or find the area of a rectangle. Measurement has enormous value as a practical skill used in everyday life; at the same time, the study of measurement can also be an opportunity for students to expand their mathematical thinking.

The cases in this *Measuring Space in One, Two, and Three Dimensions* casebook reveal how children are thinking as they work on measurement ideas. An analysis of the children's work provides a vehicle for examining the conceptual bases for measurement. Since the cases span grades K–7, they also illustrate the way children's ideas expand over the years.

One important element of measurement that children must work through is that a single object has more than one aspect which can be measured. For instance, consider a rectangle; we can measure its perimeter, its area, and the length of its sides. In order to answer the question "How big is this rectangle?" we must decide what aspect to measure. With three-dimensional objects, there is also volume to consider.

The relationships among all these measures can be puzzling. How is it possible that the perimeter of a square is a smaller number than the number that represents its area? Given two boxes, how can it be that the one with more volume actually has the smaller surface area? Working through children's thinking about questions like these is part of understanding what it means to measure in one, two, and three dimensions.

As children begin to measure, they need to determine what unit of measure is appropriate and also how to use those units efficiently to determine a measurement. An integral part of this work is learning how to visualize the space that is to be measured—how to break it into parts and to see how those parts are related to one another and to the whole. For example, underlying the process of finding the area of a rectangle is the idea that we can divide it into rows and columns; underlying the process of finding the volume of a box, that we can see it as layers, slices, or stacks. Analyzing the children's thinking provides insights into this process of decomposing and recomposing space. These insights lay the groundwork for examining how the area of a triangle (or a trapezoid, or a parallelogram) can be compared with that of a rectangle, a process that leads to the development of formulas for area.

Through the *Measuring Space in One, Two, and Three Dimensions* casebook and seminar, you will explore issues of measurement and how children in elementary and middle school come to understand them. The cases were written by elementary and middle school teachers recounting episodes from their own classrooms. All had inclusive classrooms; the range represents schools in urban, suburban, and rural communities. The teacher-authors, who were themselves working to understand the "big ideas" of the elementary and middle-grade mathematics curriculum, wrote these cases as part of their own process of inquiry. They came together on a regular basis to read and discuss one another's developing work.

The cases are grouped to present children in classrooms who are working on similar mathematical issues related to measurement. Through the cases, you will study children's initial ideas as they talk about how big their foot is or which box is bigger; you will discover the cognitive work involved in structuring space in one, two, and three, dimensions; and you will see children applying their understandings at ever-greater levels of abstraction.

In the cases in chapter 1, children measure or compare objects and consider different aspects of size: length, width, height, area, and volume. Chapter 2 explores a skill at the heart of measurement: decomposing and recomposing space in one, two, and three dimensions. Chapters 3–6 explore the measure of length, area, and volume; they draw on previous chapters to point out connections among ideas. Chapter 7 is devoted to the complicated relationships between area and perimeter and between surface area and volume.

Chapter 8, the last in the casebook, is the essay, "Highlights of Related Research"; it summarizes some recent research findings that touch on the issues explored in the cases (chapters 1–7).

C H A P T E R

1

Different aspects of size

From early on, children are interested in questions of size: Who is the biggest child in the class? Who gets the biggest piece of cake? Straightforward though these questions may sound, it is not always clear what we mean when we ask, "How big is this object?" or "Which of these two objects is bigger?" In fact, there are many ways to look at size and size comparisons. Is this object longer than another? taller? wider? Does it cover more area? Does it contain more volume? We are sometimes surprised to discover that, looked at one way, this object is bigger; but looked at another way, it's smaller.

In this first chapter of *Measuring Space in One, Two, and Three Dimensions*, we watch children investigate different aspects of size. Some explorations start with a question about measuring: How would you measure a puddle? How big is your foot? If we wanted to know how big this part of the rug is, how would we figure it out? Other explorations grow out of the challenge to compare objects, for example, by ordering a set of rectangles or containers, or by comparing the size of two boxes.

Through the children's explorations, we can examine these aspects of size ourselves and begin considering exactly what children must learn about them. What do the children in these cases bring to their inquiries? What do they discover? And what have they yet to learn? As you read this chapter, identify one place in each case where a child has worked through, or is in the process of working through, an issue about measurement. What is that issue?

C A S E 1

Many methods for measurement

GRADES 1 AND 2, MAY

I teach a first- and second-grade combination class. Over the past year, we have studied measurement as it integrates with social studies or science. Recently I ran across a good measurement problem to be used for assessment. I decided to try it to determine how many different ideas my students have about possible ways to measure. This was the question: How would you measure a puddle?*

TEACHER: First of all, what is a puddle?

LAKEAH: It's kind of like mud.

KRISTINA: It's like a little lake on the ground.

*From J. Westley, *Puddle Questions: Assessing Mathematical Thinking* (Mountain View, CA: Creative Publications, 1994).

Measuring Space in One, Two, and Three Dimensions

Mary

NORIKO:	It's like when it rains, but not enough to flood.
JOSH:	A source of leftover rain.
TEACHER:	I want you to look at the things on this table [a sponge, a cup, a ruler, a tape measure, yarn, cubes, and a spoon]. Do they give you any ideas about how you might go about *measuring* a puddle?
JENNY:	Do you mean how deep it is, or how far it is around?
TEACHER:	You could think about measuring the puddle in both of those ways. Is there anyone who already has an idea about how to measure a puddle?
KRISTINA:	Cubes. I would lay them down in a row across the puddle and count them from tip to tip.

After the children shared a few more ideas orally, I wanted them to put their ideas on paper. I told them they should use words, pictures, or numbers to explain their thinking. I also reminded them to organize their work.

When the children were ready, we came together to discuss their ideas. We sat in a circle with the sponge, cup, tape measure, and other measuring tools placed in the middle. Sue, Jonathan, and Jenny said they would measure *around* the puddle.

SUE:	I would put inch sticks around the puddle.
JENNY:	I would use a tape measure because it bends.

Jonathan presented his drawing (see Figure 1). He told us he would measure heel-to-toe around the puddle. Then he would compare the length of his foot to a "real" foot (as designated by a ruler) and find out how big the puddle was. He said he would probably use a tape measure to figure this out.

TEACHER:	Is there another way to measure the puddle besides going around the outside?
NORIKO:	Measure the height.
TEACHER:	How?

Mary

<small>GRADES 1 AND 2, MAY</small>

Noriko used her hands and a yardstick to show how she would find out how deep the water was. We talked about how to figure out the water level of a body of water. Kyle shared a similar idea in his work (see Figure 2), using a metric ruler to find the puddle's depth.

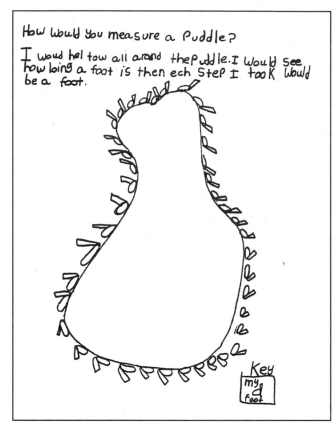

Figure 1 Jonathan shows how he would measure a puddle.

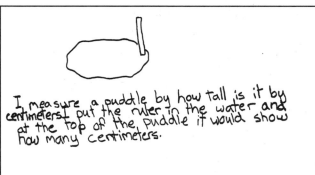

Figure 2 Kyle's work focuses on finding the depth of a puddle ("how tall is it?").

<small>8</small>   Measuring Space in One, Two, and Three Dimensions

Mary

Grades 1 and 2, May

We were ready for another measurement strategy, and Josh volunteered his technique.

JOSH: How big it is.

TEACHER: Explain "big."

JOSH: The length of it. Take some string, put it across the puddle, then hold it up to a ruler.

SEAN: I did length, but I did cubes. I would put cubes along the side of it and since the cubes are inches, just count the cubes.

Chloe offered yet another measurement strategy.

CHLOE: Weigh it.

TEACHER: How?

CHLOE: Put the water in a cup.

TEACHER: What if it doesn't fit in a cup?

CHLOE: Get a bigger cup.

ALLISON: But the cup will make it weigh, too.

TEACHER: What can we do about the cup?

KRISTINA: We should use a really light cup.

TEACHER: Any other ideas about what we could do about the cup?

JENNY: I would weigh the cup, then the water and the cup, and take away the weight of the cup. [*Wow! Big idea.*]

NORIKO: But I don't think it will work, because some of the puddle will still be on the ground.

CHLOE: I would use a sponge to get every drop.

In Chloe's written work (see Figure 3), she demonstrates her flexibility by listing five measurement strategies.

I was very pleased with the variety and depth of ideas the children had about measurement. We spent some time talking about when you would want to use a straight stick, and when something that curves (tape measure, yarn) would work better to measure a distance. This was a discussion we'd had before, and I was pleased to see that the idea was included in their thought processes.

75

I was particularly intrigued with the discussion about weight. No one brought up the idea of volume: seeing how many times a cup could be filled with puddle water. Instead, they just wanted a bigger cup to hold it all. I would like to try some volume activities in the future.

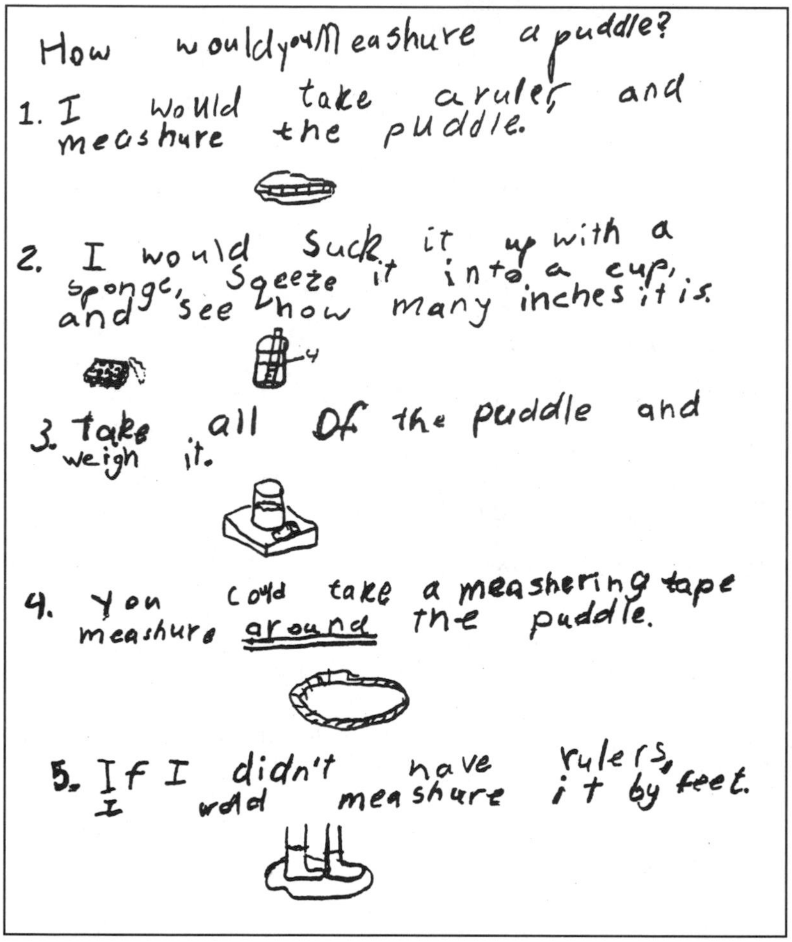

Figure 3 Chloe's ways to measure a puddle address several aspects of size.

CASE 2

My foot is nine miles

Barbara

Kindergarten, February

The children in my class often speak of the bigness of things. When asked to share their ideas about *why* they are calling something big, they apparently have not yet developed the language they need to support their exclamations of how big or how small things look.

Lately the children have been tracing their feet and cutting out the resulting paper foot shape. As they work in the rug area, there is a constant buzz of conversation. Because of their varying skills in tracing and cutting, the feet they produce vary greatly in size, from feet that would fit a giant to feet that would fit a mouse! There are also many examples of more accurate sizes in between. The vast differences in these paper feet have stimulated the children to discuss size (bigness and smallness). When I ask why they think their foot is big or small, they say:

"It looks big."

"I wear a size 7."

"Look at it."

"Mine is big; his is small."

"Big. Me big."

I decide to use their interest in their feet and in "bigness" to begin some activities with measurement. We have not formally explored measurement concepts, so I am curious to find out how the children will approach a measurement activity.

I mention that we will spend some time measuring the children's traced feet. They are pretty excited about this. We gather on the rug, and I explain that I will trace one foot for each of them. Then they can use anything they want in the room to measure their foot, however they want to do it. When I mention the measuring part, a few children speak of needing a measuring tape.

TEACHER: What's a measuring tape?

TAMMY: What you measure stuff with.

TEACHER: You measure stuff with a measuring tape. But what is it?

TAMMY: It's a tool that measures things so you know if it is big or   110
           small.

ELLEN: I have one at home. My dad used it to measure me.

TEACHER: I don't have a measuring tape at school.

ELLEN: I can bring mine in tomorrow.

TEACHER: Let's try to use things in the classroom to measure our feet.   115

One by one, I trace each child's foot and send the class off to begin
measuring. They have the run of the classroom and free access to all the
materials. Ellen immediately heads to the connecting cubes. Yusi quickly
follows her and begins his work. Oscar, who is relatively new to our class
and does not yet have a good command of the English language, sits   120
down at a table and uses a magnifying glass to look at his foot. I think he
is confusing the ideas of measuring and exploring. Well aware of his
actions, I decide not to interrupt his exploration at this time. I am not
ready to tell the children what to do; instead, I want to see where they
will go with this activity by themselves, so I purposely let Oscar continue   125
with his own decisions.

After everyone's foot is traced, I start to move about the room to see
what is going on. I notice that many children are wandering aimlessly,
holding their paper, clearly without any idea how to start. I explain that
they have a copy of their foot, and that they can use anything they want   130
to find out "how big" their foot is, but this does not help anyone. At this
point, I gather the children for a quick discussion of what it means to
measure. I ask, "What does it mean to measure your foot?"

I'm met with total silence from the whole group, along with some very
confused and disengaged looks. What am I getting into? I struggle,   135
quickly, with the choice of letting them go ahead alone to see what they
will do, or giving them some instruction and a place to start. Generally,
my inclination is to let them struggle through on their own, but their body
language and facial expressions clearly tell me that I need to approach this
differently. I hold up one of their papers with a traced foot on it.   140

Barbara

KINDERGARTEN, FEBRUARY

TEACHER:	There are lots of ways to measure things. Ellen has started to measure her foot by going from the top to the bottom [*with my hand, I motion along the length of the foot*]. There are lots of other ways to find out how big your foot is. For example, you can …

Suddenly, there is a burst of excitement in the room. Several children have ideas.

ROCKY:	You can go around the sides.
ABIGAIL:	You can do a side.
MICHAEL:	I know. You can look at the inside.
TEACHER:	There arc lots of different ways. Give it a try.

At this point, the children start to move around the room with more purpose and energy. I think, "Whoa! What just happened?" As I continue to circulate, I notice several interesting things about measuring.

Ellen has confidently placed cubes on her traced foot, from the middle of her heel up to the middle toe, with cubes hanging over the edges of the shape at each end. I ask her how big her foot measures. She counts her cubes and says, "Ten inches." I leave Ellen to record her work (see Figure 4). When I return later, she says, "Actually, it is nine." When I ask why, she reports, "I had to take one away. It was too big. The cubes went too far."

Yusi uses cubes in a similar way, but his cubes make a more erratic line, with many cubes extending beyond the toe and heel. He notices this on his own and says, "Oops, not here." When I ask why, Yusi motions to the area on the paper that is not his foot and says again, "Not here." He fixes the cubes. When I ask him how big his foot measures, he says, "Ten feet." English is not his first language, and I think that his use of the word *feet* is not the measurement term, but refers to his foot.

After the class discussion, Oscar puts away the magnifying glass and joins the children with the cubes. He also places his cubes inside his traced foot, up the middle, but his cubes reach the traced lines exactly, not spilling over at all. When I approach him, he offers, "I found out nine foots." He has used nine cubes.

I ask Oscar, "How big is your foot?"

Barbara

Figure 4 Ellen measured her traced foot with cubes placed end to end.

He says, "My foot is nine miles." He points to his real foot and says, "Big. Bigger." 175

Michael has covered his entire traced foot with wooden inch cubes, not attending to the outline. I ask, "How big is your foot, Michael?"

He says, "16 pounds." This number matches the 16 blocks he used to cover up the foot shape. 180

Maletu also fills in his foot, but uses pompom balls. The basket has pompom balls of varying sizes. He uses six of the biggest ones and one smaller one. They do not completely fill the space, but they are spread out all over the place: in the foot, outside the foot, all around.

TEACHER: How big is your foot? 185

MALETU: I grow.

TEACHER: Yes, you are a big boy. What did you find out about your foot?

MALETU: Here is my foot.

TEACHER: I see that you used pompom balls. How many did you use? 190

MALETU: I count seven.

TEACHER: How big is your foot?

MALETU: My shoe.

Measuring Space in One, Two, and Three Dimensions

Barbara

KINDERGARTEN, FEBRUARY

Rocky brings his paper over to me. I did not see him do the actual measuring, and from his paper, I cannot tell what he did, but I can read that he wrote, "My foot is 2 feet across." He tells me that he used the game pieces. I still have no idea what he is talking about or how he has measured. I convince him to do it again so I can watch.

Rocky gets out some of our smallest geoboards and places them around the outside of his foot. The placement is not tidy—the boards overlap a lot and are crooked—but they do sort of fit around the perimeter. He uses six boards to fit all the way around. On his paper Rocky has drawn only five of the boards, but writes that his foot is two feet across. When he finally explains all this to me, he points to the two geoboards that go up the side of his foot and calls that the "two feet across" part.

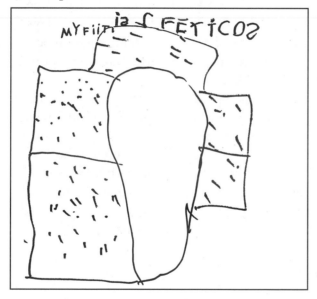

Figure 5 Rocky surrounded his foot with plastic squares and called this measure "2 feet across," referring to the two squares along the length.

Needless to say, I am impressed, surprised, and stimulated by all the work. Many of the children do have ideas about measuring. But what was going on for them? They showed excitement about measuring, and they shared some conventional ideas. Initially, they were puzzled when given the chance to measure, but they were able to offer ideas when given an example. They used terms such as *inches, feet, miles,* and *pounds.* Some of them "fixed" their work to stay within boundaries. Most of them used only one kind of object in their measuring. It is a good starting place. As the year continues, it will be interesting to see what the children do with their developing ideas about measurement.

Sizing up the meeting area

Isabelle

GRADE 2, FEBRUARY

There is a rectangular carpeted section of the floor in my second-grade classroom we call the "meeting area," and we use it in a variety of ways. Sometimes we sit in a circle, such as during Morning Meeting. At other times, such as Read-Aloud Time, the children sit in informal rows. When we're counting to the "daily number," keeping track of how many days we've been in school, the children sit in a horseshoe facing the number line. At other times of the day, children use the area to read with a partner or work with a small group.

We often struggle to fit all 20 second graders into the meeting area in a way that affords enough "personal space." It looks plenty big until we're all trying to sit there together. One February day, I decided the meeting area would pose an interesting context for some work with area and measurement. When the children were gathered, I reminded them about the various ways we use this area. I told them I often wonder about the size of the space, and I invited them to think about that with me. I asked, "If we wanted to know how big this part of the rug is, how would we figure it out?"

KEITH: I think it's 20 feet.

TEACHER: How do you think about that, when you say 20 feet?

KEITH: Because from Eddy all the way up to the number line, well, there's half of the class right here [*he motions from Eddy halfway around the horseshoe*], and there's half of the class right here on the other side [*now he motions from Eddy halfway around in the other direction*].

I quickly drew Keith's idea on chart paper.

Isabelle

GRADE 2, FEBRUARY

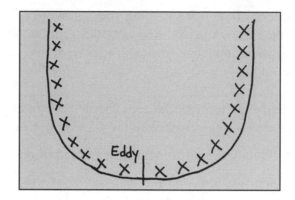

TEACHER: So are you saying that you're using the people in the horseshoe to measure?

KEITH: Yes.

TEACHER: Any other ideas about how we could find out how big this area of the rug is?

FIONA: Well, I think it might be like two yardsticks.

TEACHER: Could you say a little bit more?

FIONA: I think there could be like one yardstick right here, and another yardstick over there [*she points across the horseshoe*]. And then that would be two yardsticks. And then going this way [*she draws a line in the air perpendicular to the first*], there would be two yardsticks.

At this point, I went to get Fiona a meterstick with inches marked on one side, explaining that I didn't have a yardstick but this would work just as well. I asked her if she could show us what she meant.

FIONA: I mean, put the yardstick from the middle over to there. [*She lays the stick across the horseshoe, reaching from one edge into the empty center.*]

When Fiona referred to the meterstick as a yardstick, as did her classmates for the rest of the lesson, I chose not to correct the language because I didn't want to interrupt the train of thought.

TEACHER: I wonder how that's helping you figure out how big this part of the rug is. You said two yardsticks, and you've put that yardstick down one time. Show us what two yardsticks would be. 265

Fiona used her finger to mark the spot where the yardstick ended, then moved the beginning of the yardstick to the spot being held by her finger.

TEACHER: And then you said something about two more yardsticks?

FIONA: I meant two more yardsticks going this way. [*Again, she draws a line in the air perpendicular to the yardstick on the floor.*] 270

TEACHER: Could you take the yardstick and show us what you mean?

Fiona moved the yardstick so one end was at the number line, laying it across the horseshoe in the other direction. Again she marked the ending spot with one finger, picked up the yardstick, and moved it along so it started at the spot held by her finger. I drew another diagram on the chart paper to represent what Fiona had done. 275

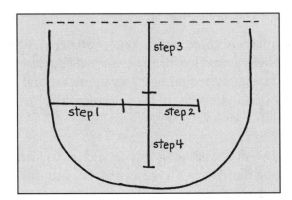

TEACHER: Are you finished?

FIONA: Yeah, but maybe one more yardstick, like three yardsticks going that way and three yardsticks going that way. 280

TEACHER: But you didn't actually put the yardsticks down three times. Are you just estimating?

FIONA: Yeah.

Isabelle

When I asked for any other ideas, Roger raised his hand. Roger has a learning disability that makes it difficult for him to organize and express his thoughts clearly. He also has a difficult time sequencing numbers and letters visually. As a result, I often need to listen extra hard and to help him clarify his ideas.

ROGER: [*He places one end of the stick near the number line.*] See, it would be right here. Then you could move it down right here [*he marks the end of the stick and moves it another length*]. And then there would be a little piece left at the end. Then you could count it.

I drew a sketch of Roger's idea:

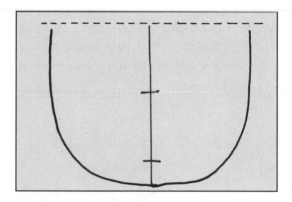

TEACHER: So you're noticing the piece that didn't get measured, and to you it doesn't seem like a whole yardstick?

ROGER: Then you could add on the little piece, and I know how much it is altogether.

TEACHER: What would you say it is altogether?

ROGER: Almost 100.

TEACHER: Almost 100 what?

ROGER: Meteors.

TEACHER: Meters?

ROGER: Yeah.

TEACHER: And how do you get 100?

ROGER: Two big ones almost make 100, plus a little one at the end.

TEACHER: Where does the 100 come from? What are you noticing that makes you say 100? Is it those little numbers on the stick?

ROGER: Yeah, I count another 83 up.

Two things were getting in Roger's way here. First, the numbers on the ends of the meterstick were covered by metal hanging plates. Second, he was looking at the numbers upside down. Thus he read 38 as 83.

TEACHER: I think you're looking at that number upside down. Look over at the other side of the stick—now, what's that number?

ROGER: 38.

Roger seemed concerned with making Fiona's method more accurate. I decided to check in with the rest of the class to see if anyone could paraphrase what Roger had said so far. Tracy volunteered.

TRACY: I think he's saying it's 38 inches across the yardstick. That's all I heard.

TEACHER: Roger, can you help Tracy with the rest?

ROGER: Because another 38 is close to 100.

TEACHER: Roger, are you saying that there would be a little left over, so you're estimating it's 100?

ROGER: Yeah, and you can use the numbers to count up the rest.

TEACHER: So it sounds like you want to use the numbers on the yardstick, and add them together to find how many it is?

ROGER: Yeah.

Roger had struggled to organize his thoughts, and much of what he said had come out in bits and pieces. I sensed that most of his classmates had been struggling to grasp what he was thinking. I also had to restrain myself, helping him just enough to get his thoughts out while protecting his ownership of those ideas at the same time.

TEACHER: I think we have enough listening energy left for one more person to share their thinking.

GABRIELLE: 20 feet.

TEACHER: Where do you get 20 feet?

GABRIELLE: Because it's not about the horseshoe. Do you know how we sit in rows when you read? Well, we take up all the rug by making three rows.

TEACHER: So you're noticing that when we sit on the rug in three rows, we seem to fill that space with 20 people.

GABRIELLE: Yeah, and sometimes we make a fourth row. Sometimes the fourth row doesn't have a lot of people. It just has four or something.

I drew the four rows to illustrate Gabrielle's thinking:

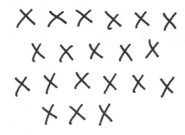

Gabrielle was recalling that, depending on how the children arrange themselves, we have from five to seven people in the first three rows. Occasionally we have a fourth row that doesn't seem quite full. There was no response to Gabrielle's idea, other than some wiggling bodies. Finally, Tanya raised her hand.

TANYA: What Gabrielle is saying… I don't know how that could help us figure out how big this part of the rug is.

GABRIELLE: Because there's 20 people on the rug, and we fill up the whole rug, and so it might be 20 feet.

TEACHER: So you're saying every person would stand for a foot? What do you think about that Tanya?

TANYA: I don't know what I think about it.

TEACHER: We're going to leave it there for now. Let's take another look at the four different ways that people had to think about it.

340

345

350

355

360

We stopped there and wound up the discussion by looking back over my sketches on the charts.

I've become interested in what children pay attention to when they set out to solve a problem. Keith seemed to be looking at the boundaries of the space. Fiona and Roger looked at the space inside the boundaries and seemed to think about each dimension (what I'll call the length and the width) separately. Gabrielle was using the way we fill a space as a measurement of its size. I think it's interesting that Gabrielle's idea drew the only negative reactions. Tanya was able to express her confusion, but judging from the nodding heads that accompanied her comments, Tanya wasn't the only one who didn't know what to think about Gabrielle's idea.

365

370

CASE 4

Rectangles and chocolate bars

Olivia
GRADE 3, JANUARY

My job this year is to help my colleagues implement *Investigations in Number, Data, and Space*, a curriculum new to our school. This means that I periodically work through a single set of lessons with several different classes. In January, I presented the activity "Ordering Rectangles."* Although I worked with three different third-grade classrooms, the conversations were strikingly similar, so I'll write them up as though I worked with a single class.

375

For this activity, pairs of students are given a set of seven rectangles, with dimensions running from 1 to 8 inches. The rectangles are lettered for identification purposes. Partners work together to put the rectangles in order, from the biggest to the smallest. These terms are not defined for

380

---

*From J. Akers, M. Battista, A. Goodrow, D. Clements, and J. Sarama, *Shapes, Halves, and Symmetry*, a grade 2 unit of *Investigations in Number, Data, and Space* (Glenview, IL: Scott Foresman, 1998).

them. Students are left to determine for themselves what is meant by "biggest."

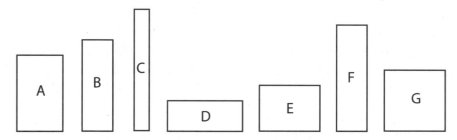

DAY ONE, THE ORDERING RECTANGLES ACTIVITY

I began the activity by telling the students to cut out their rectangles and order them from biggest to smallest, discussing the order with their partner. When both partners agreed, they were to paste the rectangles in this order on a piece of construction paper. I explained that when everyone was finished, the class would come together to share what each pair had found. The students eagerly set to work. From my observations, partners worked well together and relatively quickly agreed on an order for the rectangles.

After this first step, the students were anxious to come together to share their work. All were eager to find out which pairs had "gotten it right." I explained that I was not going to give an answer, and that later we would be working together on another activity to help us think about the size of the rectangles. Saying this seemed to make the students feel less competitive and more relaxed about sharing their answers.

As the students came to me, either in pairs or individually, I wrote their sequences on chart paper. As I had seen previously when doing this activity with other classes, all the students had characterized C as the biggest rectangle.

TEACHER: Everyone picked C as the biggest rectangle. What is it about C that made you call it the biggest?

DAVID: It's the longest rectangle.

I asked if other students agreed with David's description of C and received many affirmative responses. However, I wondered what they meant by the term *longest*. Was it really length that they were paying attention to? I turned rectangle C on its side.

385

390

395

400

405

410

TEACHER: If I turn C like this [*sideways*], is it still the longest rectangle? [*Many murmured yeses and nodding heads.*] If it's turned on its side, would you still call it the biggest rectangle?

The response to this question was much less definitive. Many students looked confused. I could hear replies of "I don't think it would be the biggest anymore."

TEACHER: It sounds like many of you don't think C would be the biggest if it is turned sideways. So what is it about C that makes it the biggest if it is standing up like this? [*I turned it back so that the letter C had the proper orientation.*]

YASMINE: If it's that way, it's the tallest.

Yasmine's use of the word *tallest* to describe C resulted in looks of relief from much of the class. Many chimed in their agreement. In fact, from the sequences I had recorded, clearly most students had taken height as the determining factor for "bigness."

TEACHER: It sounds like one way to tell which is the biggest is to look at how tall the rectangles are.

There were many yeses and nods. When I asked the class what else they observed about the sequences I had recorded, a number of hands went up. I called on Kateria.

KATERIA: All of us had C, F, and B as our first three rectangles.

When I asked her why she thought that that was true, she replied that they were the three tallest rectangles. I asked about other observations.

ROBERTO: More of us put the order as C, F, B, A, D, G, E than any other way [*see Figure 6*].

Roberto was correct. Interestingly, this was the most common order predicted by the *Investigations* authors. Students who picked this order had changed the orientation of rectangles D and E (as the side-turned letters show) and had used height as the number one factor in determining size. (As I write this case, I am aware of missed opportunities for pushing my

415

420

425

430

435

440

students' thinking. I don't recall asking why they decided that A was "bigger" than D when both rectangles have the same height, and why G was "bigger" than E where the same holds true. In fact, two groups had placed D before A. Had I questioned the students about how they made these choices, I could have triggered an acknowledgment of the need to consider width as well as height when determining overall size.)

445

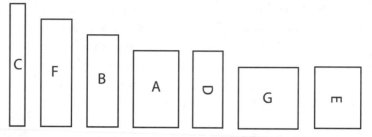

Figure 6 This is the "biggest-to-smallest" order that most students chose, with rectangles D and E turned on end.

Time was running short. When I asked for more observations, someone noted that C, F, B, A, G, E, D was the second most popular order chosen (see Figure 7). Students who sequenced their rectangles this way had maintained the original orientation (with the letters D and E upright), but still made height the main factor in determining size.

450

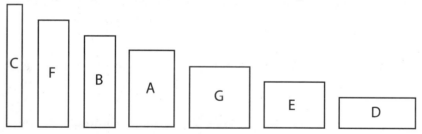

Figure 7 When rectangles D and E are not turned on end, ordering by height results in a different "biggest-to-smallest" order.

Our time was up for the day. I told the students that the next day, we would look more deeply into the question of what makes one rectangle bigger than another.

As I thought about my experiences doing the "Ordering Rectangles" activity with these classes, I was struck by how remarkably similar the results and discussions had been. In all three classrooms, students had looked at the "tallness" of each rectangle as the way to determine relative size. The two sequences illustrated here were the most commonly

455

selected, depending only on how the students had oriented D and E. What made *height* so compelling to all these students?

I pondered this question before moving on to the "Covering Rectangles" activity the next day, and a couple of thoughts came to mind. First, most students in these classes had not been introduced to, or had not explored, the concept of area. While a couple of students in one class had made reference to the "space inside" a four-sided figure, I don't remember that any other students ever raised the idea of the space inside the rectangles. My second thought was about our society's fascination with height. When we talk about which student in a class is the biggest, for example, we typically base this on height. Doesn't it make sense, then, that young students often think of *big* and *tall* as synonymous?

DAY TWO, THE COVERING RECTANGLES ACTIVITY

The follow-up activity for the second day is "Covering Rectangles," which challenges students to think about the idea of size in a deeper way. Now the students are asked to imagine that the same rectangles (A-G) are chocolate bars. The question of which candy bars would have the most chocolate encourages the students to focus on more than just the height of the rectangles.

Before introducing this activity, I wanted the students to think about other ways that they might define *biggest*. I asked once again about their unanimous selection of C as the biggest rectangle.

SHAMIKA: Well, C is the tallest rectangle, so I think that it must be the biggest.

I asked the students if they thought the tallest thing would always be the biggest. My question was met with a number of confused looks and some murmured expressions of uncertainty.

TEACHER: What if two people walked into this room, and one of them was tall and thin, and the other person was shorter but very wide. Which person would you say was bigger?

JASON: The shorter person could weigh more, so maybe you could say that that person was the biggest.

BRENT: I think Jason's right. Maybe the tallest doesn't always mean biggest.

I told the class that we were going to look at the rectangles again to see if there was another way to think about their size. I explained that when mathematicians talk about the size of rectangles and other shapes, they sometimes think about the space inside of these shapes. | 495

TEACHER: Mathematicians call the space inside of these rectangles the *area* of the shapes. One way for us to think about the area of these rectangles is to imagine that they are candy bars, and to | 500 think about how much chocolate each bar would have.

I said that when I was a little girl, every time my grandfather came to visit, he would bring my sister and me each a giant-sized chocolate bar. When we took the wrappers off these bars (which the students agreed were rectangles), we could see that they were made up of many small | 505 squares of chocolate. I suggested that the color tiles we use for other activities are similar to those small squares of chocolate, and I asked the class how we could use the tiles to figure out how much "chocolate" each rectangle/candy bar contained.*

MARISOL: We could put the tiles on the rectangles to see how many we | 510 need to cover each one.

The other students thought Marisol's idea was a good one. They were anxious to begin. However, before they started the activity, I was curious to see if talking about size in this way had already changed their perception of which bar was the "biggest." | 515

TEACHER: We are going to do what Marisol suggested, but first, do any of you have a prediction about which candy bar will have the most chocolate? You all thought C was the biggest rectangle before. What do you think now?

The response to my question was almost immediate. So many students | 520 had answers, I can't attribute them to specific individuals:
"I think that G will have the most chocolate."

---

*Of course, the amount of chocolate would actually be measured in volume, but this was a complication my third graders didn't need to consider. If the bars are all the same thickness, the one that covers more area also contains more chocolate. The idea of comparing the amount of chocolate helped the children think about the problem.

"I think it's G, too."

"I think A is the biggest candy bar."

"I think it's A or G."

The conversation went on like this. Most students focused on G or A, with a couple of E's thrown in as well. I was surprised at the rapidity and seeming painlessness of this shift in their thinking. They didn't seem at all concerned about their prior conclusion that C was the "biggest" rectangle.

TEACHER: It's interesting that so many of you are thinking that G or A will have the most chocolate. Before, you all said that C was the biggest rectangle. Why do you think that G or A will have the most chocolate and not C?

FRANCISCO: Well, I think so because G and A are both fatter than C.

Other students agreed with Francisco. I was struck by the fact that so many of them were no longer looking at only the height of the rectangles. I would have liked to ask more questions. However, it was clear that the students were getting restless. It was time to start the activity.

The students eagerly went to work with their partners from the "Ordering Rectangles" activity. They covered the rectangles with the color tiles and carefully recorded the number of tiles needed to cover each one. They talked with their partners about how their results would change the order of their rectangles. They discussed which chocolate bar they would most like to have. Xiomara wrote that she would like G because "it is the biggest chocolate bar and I like chocolate bars a lot." Yasmine, who does not like chocolate, wrote that she would want C "because it is the smallest one."

When the students came together to share what they had found, all agreed that G was the candy bar with the most chocolate and that C, the one they had initially called the biggest, was in fact the opposite. They agreed that while B and E "looked different," each contained the same amount of chocolate. A, which many students had thought would be the biggest, was identified as having one less square than G.

One by one, volunteers got up and placed a rectangle to show the new order they had found: G, A, F, B and E, D, and finally C (see Figure 8). I was again struck that the students seemed unconcerned by the drastic change from their initial perceptions.

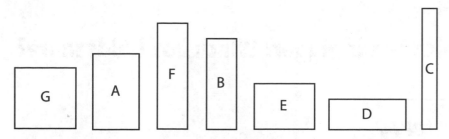

Figure 8 When students used color tiles to determine the area of the seven rectangles, they arrived at this biggest-to-smallest order.

In writing this case and reflecting on the events and discussions that took place, I am left with a number of questions. If my memory serves me, some students used interchangeably the terms "the biggest rectangle" and "the one with the most chocolate." Did they all see these two things as the same? Or was C still the "biggest" rectangle in the minds of some students, even though it didn't contain the most chocolate? I'm sure that some (and possibly many) of the students did experience a shift in their thinking about what we mean by "biggest." However, others probably did not. What could I have done to make this experience more meaningful to all students?

When I had done these same activities in a different class earlier in the year, Anita raised her hand and stated that she could prove in another way that C was not the biggest one. She had noticed that C was half the width of F. "If I cut F in half the long way and put one half on top of the other, F will be much longer than C." Anita's observation sparked a lot of interest among her classmates and led to an exploration in which students cut up the other rectangles and reconfigured them in an attempt to prove that they were all bigger than C.

No student in my current group made a similar observation. I am wondering now if I should have tried to push their thinking in this direction by encouraging them to think of other ways to prove the relative sizes of the rectangles. Anita's observation was very powerful. If a similar observation had come from me, the teacher, rather than from one of the students, would it have had the same power and meaning? I think the answer to that question is no.

560

565

570

575

580

Which box is bigger? Which box holds more?

Beverly

KINDERGARTEN, MAY

As part of math workshop this week, I put out two empty boxes for
children to consider as they worked with me in a small group. I had
thought a lot about the dimensions before I assembled the two boxes. 585
When I taped cardboard together to form the faces of each box, I
purposely constructed them without tops. My plan was to offer children
one-inch cubes if they wanted to try filling the boxes, so I made the
dimensions as follows:

    Box A: 10 inches long, 4 inches wide, and 1 inch deep 590

    Box B: 6 inches long, 4 inches wide, and 3 inches deep

The children were very curious as I set the empty boxes on the table.

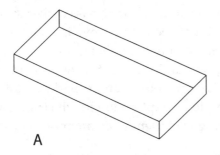 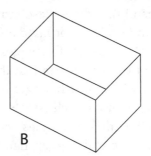

    A   B

JARED: What are we going to do with these?

TEACHER: What can boxes be used for?

MELINDA: You can put things in them, like jewelry. 595

TEACHER: Which box do you think is bigger?

Five of the six children pointed to Box B. "This one!" they chorused.

JARED: [*picking up Box A*] This one is longer.

TEACHER: How do you know which one is bigger?

MELINDA: That one [*pointing to A*] is longer. That one [*pointing to B*] is taller.

ALEX: They are bigger in different ways.

TEACHER: Which one holds more?

AMANDA: [*pointing to A*] This might.

Jared and Alex also pointed to Box A, but Ivan said he thought Box B held more. Megan also pointed to Box B. Melinda remained quiet.

ALEX: Actually, they carry the same amount.

MELINDA: Actually, they do. If this one [Box A] was folded up, it would be the same.

I was intrigued by Melinda's declaration. As she spoke, she tried to motion with her hands how you could "fold up" Box A (in half).

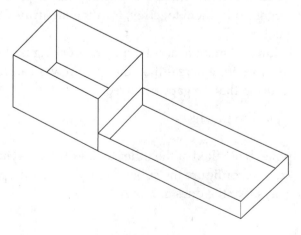

Jared moved the boxes so that their 4-inch sides were aligned.

Beverly

JARED: These [sides] are the same.

IVAN: But it's not the same length.

Ivan then moved the boxes so that their longest sides were touching.   615
He aligned the corners and motioned that Box A extended beyond Box B.

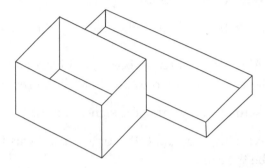

IVAN: See!

TEACHER: How could we find out which box holds more?

IVAN: By just putting them in [*he points to the basket of one-inch cubes*
            on the table].   620

The children quickly became very busy putting cubes into the two
boxes. Without much direction, they teamed up so three children were
working on each box. Melinda, Alex, and Megan worked on Box A.

MELINDA: I noticed something. This row has all green.

Indeed, as the children worked, first putting the cubes randomly into   625
the box, they began to fit them together, forming an array. One row did
have all green cubes.
    Meanwhile, Jared, Amanda, and Ivan were working on Box B. They
were piling the cubes in, whereas the other group was carefully placing
one cube at a time so that no gaps occurred.   630

JARED: This is so much!

As Jared spoke, he looked at the other box. Without saying another
word, he began to reconfigure the cubes so they filled the space exactly
and formed arrays like the ones in Box A.

32   Measuring Space in One, Two, and Three Dimensions

MEGAN: I think that one [Box B] is going to hold more.   635

JARED: I think they'll hold the same amount.

MEGAN: Maybe we can count.

These little exchanges continued while the children were filling the boxes. As the group with Box A filled in one layer, they started a second layer above the edges of the box.   640

MELINDA: We can pile them up.

ALEX: No. That's too many.

JARED: Anyway, we need more [for Box B].

Melinda did not insist on her plan, acknowledging Alex's suggestion that she was putting too many blocks in their box. Instead, she gave Jared   645
the extra blocks for the other group's box. Within a few moments, the two boxes were filled exactly to their brims.

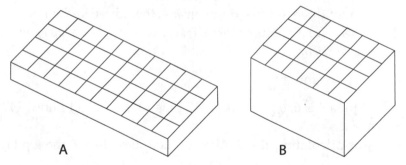

MELINDA: I think ours [Box A] has more.

TEACHER: Why?

MELINDA: 'Cause I can see more. [*She strokes her hand along the top of the*   650
            cubes in Box A.] This one [Box B] only has three in a row up.

IVAN: [*drawing his finger across a row of four cubes in Box B*] No, four.

MELINDA: Three in a row, up in the box.

Melinda was referring to the height or depth of Box B as she said "up in the box." Ivan was looking at the four cubes that went across the width   655

of Box B. Alex took a cube and placed it along the outside edge of Box B. Then he stacked four cubes up the outside, removed one, and placed his hand flat across his stack and the top of the box, saying "See, three!"

Ivan seemed to need to repeat this procedure for himself; he took three additional blocks and stacked them up against Box B, too. 660

IVAN:	This [depth of Box B] has three. That [depth of Box A] has one.
TEACHER:	How can we find out which box holds more cubes?
JARED:	We can dump them out.
ALEX:	We can take out one and test it. See, this one [Box B] has six across. I'm six! 665
MEGAN:	Ours [Box A] has ten.
AMANDA:	We have 40 [in Box A]. I counted.
JARED:	[looking at Box B] We have 24. I can't count the inside.
ALEX:	Count three. If three down inside, then three in the middle. 670 These are all pairs of three. [He puts his finger on top of one of the cubes in Box B.]
MELINDA:	Let's count.
JARED:	3 plus 3 is 6, 6 plus 6 is 12, 12 plus 12 is... I don't know, 14?

As Jared was calculating aloud, Alex counted the cubes in the top layer 675 of Box B.

ALEX:	It's 24, then two left inside.
MELINDA:	We'll dump them out.
ALEX:	No, we don't have to.
MELINDA:	I know! 1, 2, 3 [she taps one block three times with her finger, then 680 moves to a second block], 4, 5, 6.

As Melinda tried her strategy for counting, the other children chimed in. She began to lose count because some children said the numbers faster than she could. I offered my help and followed her procedure until we reached 72. 685

JARED: Wow! That one [Box A] only has 40.

MELINDA: Yeah, but if you folded it up, it would be the same.

Returning to her earlier idea, Melinda drew an imaginary line with her finger across Box A where she would fold it if she could. Her finger showed me that she saw she could divide the box in half. I saw 20 cubes on each side of her imaginary line.

TEACHER: So, which box holds more?

JARED: This one [Box B]. It has 72.

MEGAN: But 40 is more on the top.

MELINDA: I think they are the same.

This investigation with boxes elicited more conversation and thinking than I ever anticipated. How are these young children able to think and reason about the size of these boxes? When we first started talking, Alex declared that the boxes "are bigger in different ways." He is able to pay attention to different dimensions as he compares the two boxes, and the other children seem to follow this thinking.

When the children began to fill the boxes, I was amazed at the level of sophistication I saw. What prompted them to fill the boxes in neat rows, leaving no empty spaces? We certainly did not talk about this, and yet Jared shifted his group at one point to get them working more like the group that was filling Box A. Then there was the interchange about the depth of Box B. How do the children make sense of this? It is very interesting that they need to build an example *outside* the box. Also, they seem to be using something they can see about Box A in order to make sense of what they cannot see in Box B.

Finally, I think about what it means to count the actual cubes, and how that does or does not affect their thinking about which box holds more. Megan knows that there are 40 cubes on the top of Box A, and that the 40 she can see in Box A is more than what she can see on the top of Box B. Is this a beginning look at area? What does Melinda see as she speaks of folding up Box A, saying that it would then be the same as Box B? These are such complex ideas to consider. They are not easy questions, or ideas, for these children—or for me.

Exploring with containers

Rosemarie

For today's lesson, I gathered a set of six containers of different shapes and sizes for each group of four or five children. Every set included two identical containers: a black bottle cap and a cylinder. Each set was then filled out with various cups, jars, and vases—whatever I could find. | 720

When lesson time came, I explained that the task was to compare the capacities of these six containers. Each group was to put their six containers in order, from the one that holds the most to the one that holds the least, and then draw a picture of them. I gave each group a different material to fill their containers: water, sand, grass seed, beans, and rice. | 725

As they got started, at first every group just started filling their containers and worked until all were filled. I asked how they could compare which container holds more, if all the containers were filled at the same time. They then realized that they would first need to fill one, then pour the material from that container into another to see whether it overflowed or if there was room for more. | 730

As the children worked, I listened in on their conversations. First I visited the group using grass seed. | 735

MIRIAM: [*picking up a jar*] This is the biggest, largest jar. We need to fill the big glass jar completely, and then pour it into the vase. Let's start over. We can start with the biggest glass jar.

The children used a funnel to transfer the contents of the glass jar to the vase. They poured so quickly, a lot of seeds fell over the edge of the funnel. When they had emptied the jar, the vase was almost filled. | 740

GITA: The vase is the biggest container. All the seeds are poured in, but there is more room in the vase. It's not filled up.

MIRIAM: No, we have to put in all the seeds that fell out.

GROUP: [*in chorus*] Oh yeah! | 745

Rosemarie

GRADE 1, APRIL

After they had scooped up all the spilled seeds, the vase was almost full, but not to the brim. The group agreed that the vase could hold a little more than the glass jar.

At the sand table, Isaac filled up a container and compared it with the one Alberto was holding. Isaac's container was not filled up to the top when he started to pour, though he didn't notice. After Isaac emptied his container, there was still room in Alberto's. 750

ISAAC: Your container holds more than mine.

ALBERTO: It's not by much. They're almost the same.

At the water table, the group had started by arranging the containers 755 in order, from the one they predicted held the most to the one they predicted held the least. They first filled the container that they predicted would hold the most and then, using a funnel, poured that water into the next container.

TEACHER: Tell me how you decided to arrange your containers in this 760 order before filling them with water.

MELANIE: We predicted that this jar holds the most because it is widest. And just because this one is taller [*pointing to a frozen orange juice can*], it is also skinnier, so we think it doesn't hold as much. 765

COURTNEY: That's the same with this cylinder and the small black cap. The black cap is short and fat, and the cylinder is tall and skinny. I think the black cap holds more.

At the table using beans, the students were comparing a plastic cup and a small ceramic vase. 770

AYANNA: The cup holds more, because it is fatter and rounder from the top to the bottom.

TESSA: Yeah, the vase is also thick and there's not that much space inside, even though the vase is taller and looks bigger.

JULIE: Just because a container is taller, that doesn't mean it holds 775 more than a shorter container, if the short container is rounder and fatter.

Rosemarie

KJELD: Something that can be big and thick doesn't necessarily mean that it can hold more.

SAM: I think he's trying to say that because the wall of the vase is thick, it is using up some of the space inside. $\qquad$ 780

Tessa, Kjeld, and Sam were thinking not only about the height and shape of the vase, but also about its thickness. With a smaller space inside, it would have less capacity.

After the children explored for some time, I asked the groups to stop 785 what they were doing so that they could share their arrangements with the rest of us. The children sat in a circle with their group, their containers lined up in order in front of them. We first looked at all the arrangements, and then talked about what surprised us. In this follow-up discussion, the black cap and the cylinder received the most attention. 790

ALBERTO: I was surprised by the small black cap and the cylinder.

TEACHER: Tell us what was surprising to you.

ALBERTO: I thought the cylinder was bigger and can hold more. It's much taller than the black cap, but when we filled the black cap from the cylinder, there was still some space left in the 795 black cap.

VICTORIA: In our group, the black cap held more than the cylinder.

MELANIE: [*pointing to the arrangements in two other groups*] Sam, and Gita, and me don't agree that the cylinder is smaller than the black cap. 800

NELSON: The black cap held more in our group.

KJELD: I think that the black cap and the cylinder hold about the same.

Class ended before this question was resolved. In fact the cylinder, tall as it is, has less capacity than the black cap. I wonder if those children who 805 decided it holds more let some of their material spill, but didn't notice because the result fit their expectation. Tomorrow we'll look at those two containers again, perhaps as a whole class, pouring different materials from one to another. And then we can talk again about the surprising results.

2

Composing and decomposing in one, two, and three dimensions

CASE 7	Perplexing walls	*Andrea, Grade 2, October*
CASE 8	Angles, corners, and straight walls	*Andrea, Grade 2, October*
CASE 9	Arms, legs, and head—a man	*Bella, Grade 1, January*
CASE 10	I see it this way	*Josie, Grade 4, December*
CASE 11	Crazy cakes	*Phoebe, Grade 4, February*

Consider again Olivia's case 4 in chapter 1, "Rectangles and Chocolate Bars." There, third graders were ordering a set of rectangles by size. After the class had compared areas by counting the square tiles needed to cover each rectangle, third grader Anita presented a different method to show that rectangle C does not have the largest area of the set. Having noticed that C has half the width of F, she explained, "If I cut F in half the long way and put one half on top of the other, F will be much longer than C" (p. 29). In this simple and elegant move, Anita demonstrated a powerful strategy: By decomposing F into two parts and changing the position of one part, she created a new figure whose area is equal to F. Since C and the new rectangle F have the same width, she could more easily compare their areas.

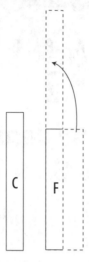

The ability to see parts of a whole and reconstruct a whole from its parts is one that we can cultivate. To do so, we need to give children opportunities to build, and to draw, and to talk about what they see. In this chapter, we read about second graders who, when asked to render comprehensible the shape of their oddly-constructed classroom, hit upon two quite different strategies: (1) decompose it into two-dimensional regions of familiar shape, or (2) carefully map its one-dimensional boundary, wall by wall, corner by corner.

In other cases, first and fourth graders start with three-dimensional structures made of cubes. In order to build accurate replicas, they analyze each structure by decomposing it into several parts. Finally, a fourth-grade class decomposes irregular polygons into parts to prove that two regions have equal area. As you read these cases, consider the following questions:

■ What are the various ways a plane figure or a solid can be divided into parts?

■ How are the parts related to one another and to the whole?

CASE 7

Perplexing walls

Andrea

GRADE 2, OCTOBER

I have spent the last few days perplexed by walls. As part of a geography unit on mapping, my intern taught a lesson on mapping our classroom. She gave students large sheets of paper and instructed them to draw the walls, from a bird's-eye perspective, to recreate the shape of the classroom, then add furniture. Earlier, I'd given these second graders several opportunities to construct physical maps of their rooms at home, the playground, and other familiar places. Initially, the assignment felt fairly straightforward, until we took a closer look at how the room is shaped. My classroom has unique dimensions because of an unusual "diagonal wall" (as my students quickly dubbed it).

5

10

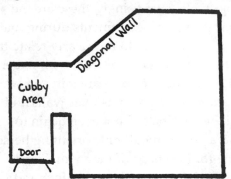

Figure 9 Andrea's second-grade classroom with its unusual diagonal wall.

Initially I took the role of observer, as this was my intern's lesson. As I watched the students begin to draw the shape of the room, I was struck immediately by the vast range in ability. One group of students clearly "got it" and seemed to work from whole to part. They were able to remain at their seats and, from their position, get an accurate sense of the dimensions and space of the whole classroom.

15

Andrea

GRADE 2, OCTOBER

Thomas approached me after he had drawn the walls for his map. "Ms. Johnson, I just figured out how to make our room bigger!" He explained his plan with an abundance of hand gestures. "If we straighten out the diagonal wall, and keep going into the cubby area, our room would be more a rectangle. It would be so much bigger!" When I asked him what shape he would actually add to our room to make the rectangle, he was quick to reply. "Kind of like a trapezoid." Not only did he have a clear image of the shape of our whole room, but he was also able to visualize the negative space, or the area that would be needed to turn our classroom into a rectangle.

Another group of students sort of got it, moving more from part to whole. This group needed to physically move themselves around the room as they assessed the space, working hard to see how the walls came together to form different shapes that make up the classroom. Zachary walked methodically around the room, drawing each wall as he passed it. This strategy made it difficult for him to relate the walls to one another. As a result, his sense of scale was greatly skewed. The diagonal wall was perplexing for this group of students, and I watched as some used yardsticks or pencils to help them to gauge the angle. For some, the diagonal wall on their map was more of a hint than a clear delineation.

Finally, a handful of students simply did not get it, and they had very few strategies to even begin the project. Not surprisingly, these are the same students who struggle with our geometry assignments during math. This assignment seemed too abstract, and they could not clearly relate the dimensions and shape of the room to anything familiar from their experiences. Evan and Will worked together and neglected to draw in any walls. Rather, they used the rectangular border of the paper as their walls and attempted to fill in the room from there. Helena did not even begin to represent the diagonal wall, and had a very difficult time orienting herself once she had drawn a large rectangle for the shape of the room. Sierra also drew a rectangle, and struggled to determine where the door and windows belonged. Ken simply sat at his desk quietly doodling.

I spent some time with Evan and Will over in the corner next to the diagonal wall, trying to help them to see the differences in angles. I asked repeatedly if they could see any familiar shapes created by the wall. They looked up at me with wide eyes, as if I were speaking a foreign language. These walls were isolated linear segments to them, and I was running out of teaching strategies to help them make the leap in understanding.

Andrea

GRADE 2, OCTOBER

I knew it was time to get more concrete. I called the "not-getting-it" group over and encouraged them to work with blocks to create their maps. The opportunity to physically manipulate the material seemed to work for most, helping them see how the walls defined the shape of the room. Helena was clearly inspired, and quickly returned to revise her original map. Evan and Will, however, still struggled. Unfortunately, our period came to an end, and we had to abandon the project for the day.

The following day I approached the entire class with my perplexing walls problem. I explained that this was a very difficult assignment, and that I had run out of ways to help students make sense of the room. I appealed to the class for assistance, asking them to describe some of the shapes they saw in the room. An enthusiastic class volunteered their responses.

Susannah saw a large rectangle created when we divided the room lengthwise. Jack saw an even larger rectangle that would include Susannah's shape if we moved the dividing line back a bit. The students decided that we should use yarn to mark the dividing lines more clearly, so I happily stapled yarn to the floor at their suggested points. Many hands were up by now, and I could hear the murmur of voices as students began to make their own connections.

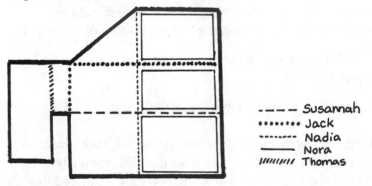

Figure 10 The lines show how the students decomposed the classroom into familiar shapes, which were highlighted by stapling yarn to the floor.

Nadia saw that the classroom could be divided into yet another rectangle, with a line running the full width of our classroom. Nora saw that Nadia's dividing line, crossing Susannah's and Jack's, created several smaller rectangles, which, when combined, created her larger rectangle. Thomas bounced up and down in his seat as he declared that the cubby area could be considered a rectangle as well. Finally, we examined the area created by the diagonal wall. A near universal cry went up, "It's a triangle!"

"And if you had another triangle just like this one, and you put them together, they would make a rectangle," explained Susannah.

Wow! Finally, many of the students had a clearer understanding of how to use shapes they knew, and how to apply this knowledge to help them to make sense of an unfamiliar space.

Evan and Will were not active participants in this class discussion, but they were attentive and appeared to be following the conversation. As the rest of the class returned to their maps, I was interested to see how much these two had followed, and if they would be able to bring any new understanding to this assignment.

Both seemed eager to return to their map drawings, which they flipped over. As they started again, I sat back, trying to let them take the lead.

WILL: Well, where do we start?

EVAN: Let's do the big rectangle near the big blackboard.

I was pleased that they had a springboard. They took a few minutes to get the paper oriented and to decide where the rectangle should be placed. Finally, they drew in a large rectangle at the bottom of the paper.

EVAN: Now I think we need to do the rectangle over by the computers.

WILL: What next? We have to have the triangle, too.

I was so thrilled! They were using these geometric shapes to describe and draw the main space in the classroom. It seemed like such a leap in understanding. Was it the yarn and class discussion that facilitated this jump? Did the concrete work with the blocks give them a base of understanding? Or was it the whole series of activities and experiences that added up to this moment?

At this point, I left Will and Evan to check on the rest of the class. When I returned several minutes later, the boys had drawn the cubby area as a small rectangle unconnected to the rest of the room. Hmmmm. Ahead three steps, back two.

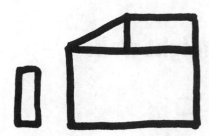

Figure 11 Will and Evan drew the room this way after hearing the whole-group discussion of shapes within the room.

This activity has raised many questions in my mind. In my teaching, I have been feeling more comfortable and competent at assessing my students' numerical thinking and number sense. I feel that I have more strategies to help them to get to the next step and begin to make those leaps in understanding. This is not always the case with geometry. I am still unsure about how to help students who lack a well-developed spatial sense. How do I support students like Evan and Will as they struggle with these geometric concepts? What can I do to help them to bridge these gaps? What precisely are they "not getting"? Is this deficiency related to a larger societal emphasis on number sense in math, and a devaluing of geometry?

I am still looking closely at the skills that enable students like Thomas to think quickly and easily about shapes. He is clearly able to compose and decompose shapes with ease. He is also able to relate unknown shapes to things that he does know. He is able to see negative space, where other shapes can fit to compose larger shapes. He recognizes that certain shapes have particular attributes. Developmentally, how do these skills fit together and build upon each other?

Angles, corners, and straight walls

Andrea

GRADE 2, OCTOBER

This past week my class has continued to draw bird's-eye-view maps of our classroom. Because of the unusual dimensions of our room, this has been a challenging task for many. Two students in particular, Will and Evan, struggled through several approaches with varying degrees of success. They appeared to benefit from the whole-class activity in which we decomposed the classroom into different, familiar geometric shapes. When these two boys could see the lines of the walls as part of larger, familiar shapes, the lines became more than isolated segments for them, and they began to get a sense of the room as a whole.

Translating this understanding to a two-dimensional map of the room was still a bit of a stretch for Will and Evan, but they were quite invested in the activity, and I felt it was important for them to be successful. When I was able to spend some time with the pair, I encouraged them to return to a more concrete approach and use geoblocks to construct their map. They were visibly relieved to set aside their drawing and enthusiastically got down to work.

I noticed several things as I watched Will and Evan work. The first was their discussion of angles. They became quite focused on the angles created where two walls meet, and this is where they began their room design. Will initially explored the room with yardstick in hand, but quickly called Evan over to corner A. He held the yardstick up to create a right triangle with the two walls.

"See!" he explained to Evan, "Where the walls meet here, they can make a triangle! The walls are straight." They quickly checked corners B and C to see if they too created triangles with the yardstick. This seemed to be a big discovery for the pair. They were using a familiar relationship to begin to analyze the shape of the room.

Andrea

GRADE 2, OCTOBER

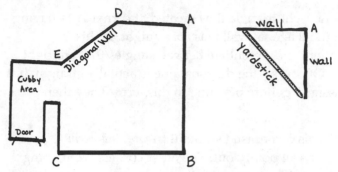

Figure 12 Exploring the space in the room, Will discovers that he can see a triangle where the walls meet.

Will and Evan chose pyramids with square bases from the block bin and placed them in corners A, B, and C to start their map. The pair then built walls to connect these pyramids. When I asked why they had chosen pyramids for their corners, they were very clear with their answers:

WILL: [*pointing to a right-angle corner on the pyramid*] See, this is like the corner here where the two walls are, where they meet.

EVAN: But the real corner's going in, not pointing out [*into the room*] like this pyramid.

The boys were very focused on the boundary of the room, examining closely the points where the walls met. Will and Evan's block map came together fairly quickly. As they constructed each new component, they would first walk through the space in the room and "measure" any corners with the yardstick. I was very interested to see how they would represent the notorious diagonal wall, which ended up being the last piece they completed. When they finally came to the diagonal wall, Will went to corner D with his yardstick, but he paused after he made his triangle with the two walls.

WILL: It's all stretched out. This triangle is open much wider than the other ones.

EVAN: I know! That's because this is the diagonal wall.

WILL: It's pointing into the cubbies. It's not straight like the others.

What do they mean by *straight*? They used the term at various points in their discussion, usually describing how two walls appear when they meet. They described the right triangle they created at corner A as having two straight lines, but the diagonal wall was *not* straight. Is this description a way for them to differentiate between angles that are right and those that are not? Of course, the diagonal line is actually straight, but it seemed they were assigning more meaning to this term. They then walked to corner E.

WILL: Hey look! This corner isn't straight! [*Again, this term "straight."*] It's all pointy out. The other corners were going in, but this one is coming out!

EVAN: That's because it has to make room for the cubbies. If the wall kept going straight, it would cut the cubbies in half.

WILL: There would be less space in the classroom. I know! If we could push this corner (E) in, the wall would be straighter, and we would have more room in our class.

Several students had made this observation on previous days, and I was unsure if Will was finally making sense of their ideas or if he had reached this understanding on his own. Either way, he was demonstrating new flexibility in his thinking about the space.

Finally, Will and Evan returned to their map to add the final pieces and create that challenging diagonal wall. After shuffling through the geoblock bin for moment, Evan pulled out a very thin triangular prism. He placed it flat on one of the triangular faces and declared the outline of the map finished. Will agreed. They still needed the three-dimensional shape of the triangular prism to define the diagonal wall in their map.

Will and Evan created a map of the room in which the exterior outline of the blocks nicely represents the boundary of the room! The boys were very proud of their work and made sure that the rest of the class had an opportunity to view their special map.

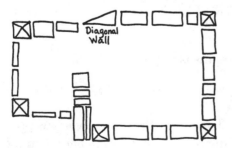

Figure 13 Will and Evan's map made of blocks, with pyramids in the corners.

Andrea

GRADE 2, OCTOBER

As I reconsider their thinking, I am interested by their shift in focus as they worked. When they began, the interior outline of the blocks represented the actual boundary for them. They were concerned that the pyramids pointed into the room rather than out; if they had been focused on the outer edge at this point, the map might have appeared accurate to them. However, at some point their focus shifted to the exterior outline, as is seen in their final representation. Was this an important shift in thinking, helping them gain a clearer understanding of the room as a whole, or was it simply easier to represent the trickier portions of the boundary through the exterior outline?

Finally, I asked Will and Evan how a teacher could help kids who had difficulty making sense of shapes. I received some wonderful advice.

EVAN: The blocks are really good to use. Drawing is too hard for me right now. I had no idea what to do or what to draw. I just didn't know where to start. And it was really hard to make the diagonal on the paper. I didn't know if the wall was going into the room, or going out. I just couldn't figure it out.

WILL: The blocks made it still challenging, but I could do it. Like, I could look with the blocks. I could take the blocks around the room, and see where those shapes were.

EVAN: The blocks also helped with the corners. The yardstick helped us think of triangles in the corners, and then we found the triangles in the [pyramid] blocks for the corners on our map.

WILL: I think that kids need lots of time to build things with the blocks and things like the pattern blocks.

As usual, I was impressed with the insight they had on their own learning. Will and Evan needed the concrete experience with the blocks to make sense of the problem in their own way and find strategies that would work for them. From there, they were able to use the things they knew, such as the shape of a triangle, to figure out what they didn't know. Will and Evan became far more confident in their work, and even though the task was still challenging, they finally had a way to understand the problem. The lack of language that I had initially sensed actually seemed directly related to self-confidence. Once they were engaged, the conversation flowed, rich in mathematical content and ideas. Even if they did

not know the conventional mathematical terms, they were able to explain
their thinking very clearly.

    I feel sure that Will and Evan would not have completed their physical
representation with the success they did if they hadn't first had plenty of
time to explore the problem. Students like Will and Evan, who have a less
developed spatial sense, seem to need lots of time to explore how shapes
work. I am faced again with the same question: How do I allow students
like Will and Evan the extra time they need when the majority of the class
is ready to move on?

CASE 9

Arms, legs, and head—a man

Bella

GRADE 1, JANUARY

I have been giving activities to my first graders to get them thinking about
how a whole is made up of parts and how those parts are related. Today I
asked them to build a simple structure from interlocking cubes, then
exchange their structures with a partner and build a copy of the structure
their partner built. When they were done, they were to draw a picture of
the structure they copied. I expected that drawing would require a deeper
level of analysis than building the copy with cubes.

    Time was short, but most of the children were able to build their struc-
tures and copy their partner's, and some were able to draw the requested
picture. Jerome and Rollins had built and exchanged structures, and
Rollins was still building a copy of Jerome's when I got over to their table.
I asked Rollins if he was having trouble, but he indicated that he wanted
to finish by himself. Jerome, however, had finished and was waiting
patiently for me to take a look at his work.

    I set out to learn about the process Jerome had followed to build a copy
of Rollins's structure and then draw his picture of it. It was after 2:00 P.M.
and almost time for the children's nap, but I felt we would have time to

review Jerome's work. (Our school day is $10\frac{1}{2}$ hours long, from 7:30 A.M. to 6:00 P.M. Nap time is necessary!) I asked Jerome about the structure that he had copied, and he told me it was a man.

Figure 14 Jerome built a copy of this cube "man" his partner made (left), then drew his picture of it (right).

| TEACHER: | How did you begin to build your structure? [*Jerome hesitated, so I decided to ask my question differently*.] What did you do first? | 275 |

| JEROME: | I measured the legs. I knew there were five. [*Jerome points to the five interlocking cubes making up the legs*.] |

| TEACHER: | How did you know that there were five? [*I want to find out what he meant by the word "measured."*] | 280 |

| JEROME: | 'Cause I counted. |

I checked the clock and looked around the room. Almost all the other children were on their mats. I was interested in pursuing this conversation, so I told Jerome that I wanted to hear more about what he did, unless he was tired and needed to take a nap. Jerome said he was fine, so I continued my questioning. | | 285

| TEACHER: | What did you do next? |

| JEROME: | I measured the arms and I got eight. Then I did the head [*he points to the tall column of nine cubes*]. It was going down. |

| TEACHER: | How did you know what number of cubes to use for the head? | 290 |

Bella

JEROME: I counted in my head, and got three for the head.

TEACHER: How did you know where to put the head?

JEROME: Because that's how Rollins had it. I looked really close. [*He places his copy next to Rollins's original structure so that they match.*]   295

Jerome's copy differed from Rollins's original only in the color of the cubes. He chose to focus on color as he went on with his description of how he built his copy.

JEROME: Four green cubes from the right to put the legs on.   300

Now we turned to Jerome's drawing. I asked him to look at the picture he had drawn and tell me the steps he took to draw it.

JEROME :   First I made the man from the leg to the head, and the head had three pieces. [*He points from the head to the left leg on his diagram.*] Then I did the other leg. Then I did the arms. [*As our conversation continues, Jerome switches his attention back and forth between the drawing and the actual cube man.*]   305

TEACHER: How many cubes did the arms have?

JEROME: [*counting the right side of the cube structure*] Four.

TEACHER: Did you check both arms in your drawing?   310

He counted the drawing of the arm on the right, and then counted the two cubes in the arm on the left. He realized that in the cube man, there were three cubes in the arm on the left.

TEACHER: What happened?

JEROME: [*looking at his drawing*] I put two!   315

He wanted to get his pencil to fix it, but I told him he didn't need to.

TEACHER: Anything else?

JEROME: The number for the leg is five.

I was curious to know how he decided where to put the second leg in his diagram.

TEACHER: Did you think about a number to attach the second leg to?

JEROME: I knew the leg had five, and it was next to the other leg, so I drew it. After I finished my picture I wrote the words.

I asked Jerome if I could keep his drawing and he agreed. It was late and Jerome needed to rest, so I sent him off for his nap.

Looking at Jerome's diagram, it seemed to me that he had drawn an L-shaped piece first (3 vertical and 5 horizontal cubes on the right). I think he began with the top of the head because he had drawn four sides for the first block and then added three lines to make the boxes below. In our conversation, he was probably giving me a description of how he saw his drawing now, rather than telling me how he actually did the work.

CASE **10**

I see it this way

Josie

GRADE 4, DECEMBER

In the activity we did today, my students used interlocking cubes to copy an image that I flashed on the overhead projector for three seconds.* I told them to try to fix the image in their mind, and then build from that mental vision. I also told them that I would flash the image a second time for them to check their work and make any needed adjustments to their cube structure. This lesson was designed to give the students experience with visual organization and analysis of images, as well as practice in communicating about 3-D drawings and structures.

---

*"Quick Images" from M. Battista and D. Clements, *Seeing Solids and Silhouettes*, a grade 4 unit of *Investigations in Number, Data, and Space* (Glenview, IL: Scott Foresman, 1998).

320

325

330

335

At first, my students expressed displeasure with the activity. They complained that three seconds would not be long enough and clearly felt I was asking them to do an impossible task. I reassured them that the second showing would really help them, giving them more than one chance. Thinking that their attitude might interfere with the task, I decided to ask first if anyone could share an experience they'd had with using a mental image to remember something. Deb mentioned the name of a local store, Faces. She said that whenever she was confused about whether the word *faces* had a *c* or an *s* in it, she remembered the sign for this store. This led to a couple more stories, and soon most students were feeling better about the task that I was asking them to do.

We spent quite a bit of time on this activity, working with eight different images on transparencies. During the flashing and building, I observed my students working with confidence even though the later images became more difficult. They were developing strategies that worked for them and applying these strategies as the images became more complex. Following are some of the strategies they shared during our discussion time.

When we talked about Image 1, Paylee explained that she saw it as three sides. Side 1 had two cubes (she called this the "front" side), side 2 had two cubes, and side 3 had three cubes. She explained that she saw both side 2 and side 3 coming off the sides of the top cube in front. I asked her how she knew which side to put the 2 cubes on and which side to put the 3 cubes on. She stated simply that she knew what side to put them on because that's the way she saw it. Did this mean she could not verbalize what she had done? When reproducing a visual image, do you need to think in such terms as *right* and *left*?

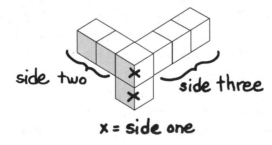

Image 1

Josie

GRADE 4, DECEMBER

Tim said he saw Image 2 as three, four, and two: three going down, four going across, and two going back. I asked him to show me the three, four, and two in his cube model, and he did, counting one cube as being in all three sections. It was interesting to me that he was able to do this without having extra cubes in his building. He was able to see not only the three, four, and two, but also that one cube was shared by these sections.

370

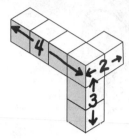

Image 2

By the way, some of my students said that Image 2 was easier. This surprised me because it was the same structure as Image 1, but turned. They didn't seem to notice this, and I decided not to bring it up at this time. Instead I put the next image on the overhead.

375

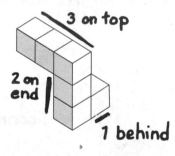

Image 3

For Image 3, Robby said he saw the top three cubes first, then saw the two "on the end" and one behind the bottom cube. I asked how he knew that last cube was behind the other two. He explained that if he could see only one whole side of a cube, then he knew it was behind a cube and not next to it. What made him notice this? Another student pointed out that Image 2 had a cube behind another in the top layer, but two sides could be seen. This discussion led others to use what were described as the *sides* of the cubes to help them recreate the buildings.

380

For Image 4, Cassie counted the number of cubes in the whole shape: six. She then explained that she saw it as two, two, and two: two across the top, two going down, then two going across again, but at the bottom. (Sounds like a crossword puzzle, but she didn't say this.) [385]

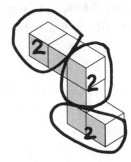

Image 4

Jasmine saw Image 5 as three at the top and two at the bottom, connected by one—a bridge in the middle. I asked how she knew which way to put the bottom and the top rows before she connected them with the bridge. She said she could remember how from her mental image, and since she remembered the way the top and bottom went, this helped her know where to put the bridge. [390]

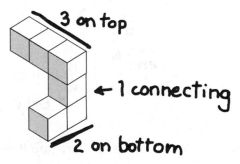

Image 5

Some students commented that Images 3, 4, and 5 were a lot alike. Each could be viewed as three top cubes and two below on the end, as Robby described Image 3. Then, in each of the three images, the last cube is in a different position. [395]

Image 6 took the most time to discuss. Some students felt strongly that this structure could have only nine cubes, while others thought it could have ten. Natalie explained that she saw three first, with two added to the [400] top end, two more going down, and two behind these. She explained that she could start with the first three and continue from that point, just adding two at a time.

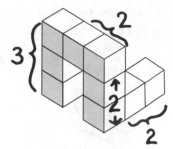

Image 6

Shaina agreed that Natalie's could be correct, but she herself had put one on the back bottom of the first three. She felt that a cube could be there and no one would see it. Robby became very interested in Shaina's idea. Using her cube building, he tried holding it at the same angle as the image on the transparency. He wanted to determine whether, from this angle, the back cube could or could not be seen. I allowed Robby and a few others to work on this, but no agreement was ever reached about this shape. In other activities we had done previously, working with silhouettes of similar cube structures, the students had discovered that a silhouette could have missing cubes in some layers, or that a different number of cubes could create the same silhouette. I was glad to see that some of my students recognized this same ambiguity in today's activity.

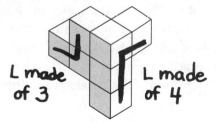

Image 7

Lisa saw Image 7 as two adjacent L's: a mini-L in the back (made up of three), connected to an upside-down L (made up of four). She made the large L first, and then just put the mini-L on the back.

Josie
GRADE 4, DECEMBER

For Image 8, Deb said she saw the square and put this together first. She then put one cube in the back on the top, and three on the bottom going off to the side. Like Lisa and her L's in Image 7, Deb was connecting parts of the image to familiar shapes. I asked if anyone else had used or seen the square when trying to build from Image 8, but no one had.

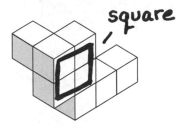

square

Image 8

Overall, a lot was discussed and a lot of different strategies were used and shared. I saw a big shift in interest from the beginning to the end of this math class. The students found many possible ways to create and interpret these images. Some were recognizing parts and chunking visual information; others were using the whole image. Some had to know how many cubes were in the whole shape. A few students recognized part of the shape as being like something else, and that became their focus. What surprised me was my students' apparent indifference to right or left orientation in their explanations. Most said, "I saw one here" or "two going back there," not "on the right" or "back to the left." They did use the terms *top, row, across, side, down,* and *behind.* Why did I notice the absence of *right* and *left*? Does it matter? What pleased me was all the critical thinking and the wide variety of strategies that were shared. I especially liked Robby's idea that cubes located behind another cube look different in the image; also Shaina's recognition that there could be a hidden cube, and some students' identifying familiar shapes in the images.

420

425

430

435

440

Measuring Space in One, Two, and Three Dimensions

Crazy cakes

Phoebe

GRADE 4, FEBRUARY

My fourth-grade students just started a fractions unit that uses an area model of fractions. In the introductory activity, students divide paper "crazy cakes" (irregular polygonal shapes) for two people to share equally.* Working with partners, they had to divide each cake and be able to prove that the resulting pieces were halves.

445

After students had finished dividing a number of cakes, we began a discussion. I picked what I expected was a fairly easy cake to divide and put it on the overhead. Elsa drew a line to show how she split it. I then turned the question to the class, "Can you prove or disprove that these are halves?"

450

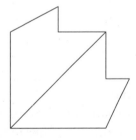

Neil said, "I know they are halves because they are symmetrical. I didn't actually fold it, but it's obvious that if I fold it on the line, the two sides would match exactly."

I remembered seeing Matthew with a different proof, so I asked him to share his. Matthew explained, "I divided it in the same place, but I have a different reason. I split the 'extra pieces' off each side to make a

455

---

*"Crazy Cakes for Two" from C. Tierney, M. Oganowski, A. Rubin, and S. J. Russell, *Different Shapes, Equal Pieces,* a grade 4 unit of *Investigations in Number, Data, and Space* (Glenview, IL: Scott Foresman, 1998).

square. I knew I could split a square into halves with this line [corner to corner]. Then I just have these two extra pieces that match. One goes with each half."

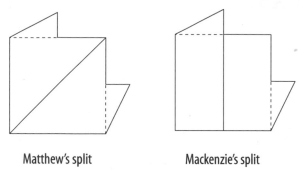

Matthew's split   Mackenzie's split

Mackenzie said, "I proved it kind of like Matthew, but I split it in a different place. I thought about the square, like Matthew did, and I split it like this [top to bottom]. Then I had the extra pieces on each half." | 460

I summarized what we had so far. "We have two different ways of splitting the cake, and two different ways of proving one of those splits. But I see one way those are all the same: You are matching regions of one | 465
half with regions of the other half. Neil exactly matched one half with the other. They are the same size and shape and fit exactly on top of each other. Matthew matched the two halves of the square with each other, and then the two extra pieces. Mackenzie did not split her cake symmetrically, but she still matched regions. She matched the two halves of the square | 470
with each other, and then the two extra pieces. If you can match the areas of the two sides, you have halves."

We moved on to another shape, and I asked Marie to show where to cut it. Marie usually lacks confidence in her mathematical ability, often prefacing any comments with, "This is probably wrong, but…." She had | 475
obviously enjoyed the crazy cake activity, though, and I had overheard her explaining it clearly to her partner during the work period. She had been excited as she found and proved her solutions. This seemed like a good opportunity for her to share something she was sure of.

Phoebe

Marie drew a single line and told us, "When I did this before, I cut the shape out. When I cut on this line, I could put the two pieces together. They were just the same." Most students had the same solution, although only a few had actually cut the pieces.

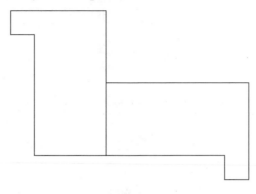

Marie's split

We worked with several other cake shapes and, as it turned out, all the solutions presented were correct, although it wasn't always obvious when they were first presented. When students solved these problems for themselves, they found only one solution and then moved on to the next problem. In our discussion, when we saw a variety of solutions for the same cake, students actually said out loud, "I never would have thought of doing it that way." This also happened when we saw a variety of proofs for the same solution. I sensed that everyone was seeing something (not necessarily the same thing) for the first time. The solutions and the strategies for proving them held a degree of novelty that kept everyone engaged.

3

Measuring length: What is a unit and how is it used?

From a very young age, children are exposed to methods and tools for measuring length, and they bring the necessarily rudimentary notions they derive from this exposure with them into the classroom. In order to use these methods and tools knowledgeably, children must sort out a number of issues, including these: What is a unit of length? What is the relationship between the size of a unit and the number of counts of that unit required to measure a given length? How are rulers used to apply units and determine counts?

This chapter spotlights children in kindergarten through grade 7 who are working on these issues. As you read, look for answers to these questions:

- What ideas do Barbara's kindergartners, before receiving any instruction, bring to the task of measuring a big box?

- What are the first, third, and seventh graders sorting out as they measure distances with their hands, feet, and paces?

- What have the second and fourth graders learned that enables them to use a ruler?

C A S E   12

A big box, books, and baskets

Barbara

KINDERGARTEN, DECEMBER

Note: Half the children in my kindergarten do not speak English as their first language, and all of these entered kindergarten without any English. There are nine different first languages spoken in my room.

My kindergarten classroom this year seems to be undergoing a never-ending process of change. Basically, we started the year in an empty space. As the year progresses, we continue to receive various supplies and necessities for the room. Every few days or weeks, something else comes in the mail for us. We have received markers, glue, connecting cubes, tables, chairs, and so much more.

It is not so unusual for us to come into the room and find a box or two waiting to be opened. Just such an event happened recently. As the children returned to the classroom from lunch, they found a very large box in the middle of the room. Tammy exclaimed, "Oh, did we get more mail?" Upon hearing that they had, the children immediately broke into cheers and began talking about what might be in the big box. They all

5

10

drew pictures and wrote some words about what they thought might be inside. On this particular day, we talked a lot about the box and what might be in it, but we did not get around to opening the box.

The next day of school, the children entered the classroom in the morning to find the box still unopened and still in the middle of the room. There were many comments and questions—mostly, "When are we going to open the box?" I assured the children that we would find time to open it that day. Their interest was high, and their excitement about the size of the box permeated the room. I decided to seize the moment and talk to the children about the "bigness" of the box.

TEACHER: A lot of people have been talking about the box. I have heard a lot of you say that the box is big. How big is the box?

At this point the children eagerly offered their ideas: Big! Really big! Very big! Super big! Very very big big! I settled them down a bit and tried to get them to take turns sharing their ideas.

ELLEN: Well, it's kind of like, half as big as the carpet.

PRABHAT: Maybe, it's half as, half as, like the... like the chart.

XIAOMING: [*pointing to the easel*] Like this.

DESMOND: The big of the box is bigger than the chair.

ROCKY: It's half of the wall.

I wondered if the children were using the phrase "half" because Ellen used it initially.

MICHAEL: [*looking around for something to say*] I think it is big, like the light.

MALETU: Maybe, like letters. [*He is actually looking at some large numbers that are on the wall.*]

MATT: The box is big—King Kong.

YUSI: Big tree.

TEACHER: The box is big, like a tree. [*Yusi agrees, that is what he was saying.*]

Barbara

KINDERGARTEN, DECEMBER

At this time, Danita returned from the bathroom and passed the box on her way to the rug. Fong yelled out, "Box bigger, Danita not bigger." I asked Danita to stop and stand near the box so that everyone would have a chance to see what Fong was seeing. The children agreed that the box was bigger than Danita. Fong got up and stood near the box, too. The children chimed in that the box was also bigger than Fong.

I decided to push the conversation, to see whether and how the children would be able to describe the bigness of the box with some measurement ideas. What does it mean to be big? What would they use to figure out its bigness? I wasn't sure the children were ready to tackle this, but I decided to forge ahead. Measurement conversations and activities so far this year had been limited, but again, I felt I could build on their excitement about this box and begin to explore some measurement ideas.

I stood up to point to the box and the children yelled out, "Ohhh, you are bigger than the box." They were clearly tuned into size comparisons. At this time, one child mentioned that Oscar was bigger than the box, too. Oscar, a large child, was new to our classroom. On this particular day Oscar was absent, so we were not able to confirm that he was bigger than the box, but it was a great observation and idea. I proceeded.

TEACHER: How tall is the box? How can we measure the box?

DESMOND: It is very, very long.

TEACHER: How can we measure it? Measuring can tell us how tall the box is. How can we measure the box?

ROCKY: With a measuring line.

TEACHER: What is a measuring line?

ROCKY: They're plastic and has numbers on it.

TEACHER: A plastic measuring line. I don't have one at school. We should probably use something we have at school.

ELLEN: I have a tape measure at home.

TEACHER: What could we use to measure this at school?

In response to my question, Xiaoming pointed to a bunch of stuff around the room. I asked him to use some words, and he said that if he took the books out of the baskets, he could use the baskets. I encouraged him to show us what he meant.

Barbara

Enthusiastically, Xiaoming proceeded to take books out of plastic baskets and wicker baskets. The rest of us watched eagerly. Xiaoming brought the different baskets over to the box and began stacking them on the floor right next to the box. Three plastic baskets nested into each other. He placed a wicker basket on top of the plastic ones and held another wicker basket on top of his stack. By now, the stack reached about a quarter of the way up the side of the box. He said, "No, big." I think he was saying that the stack was not big enough or tall enough yet.

Xiaoming looked around the room and said, "I know. Put chair here." Once again, I encouraged him to go ahead. The rest of the class sat riveted in place—I believe partly because this was interesting, but also because Xiaoming was taking the classroom apart! He moved the chair over and recreated his stack of baskets on the chair. Now there was an uproar in the room. The children were yelling and shouting that the stack was now higher than the box!

FONG: It too big! It too big!

TEACHER: It is too big?

FONG: Box is too little [*meaning, the stack is now taller than the box*].

I invited Fong to go and help out Xiaoming. At this point, all the children were moving about, scooting closer and closer to the box, probably wanting a turn to be involved. Fong and Xiaoming took one of the wicker baskets off the stack, but that made the stack too short again. Everyone tried to figure out what the boys could add to the stack so it would just reach the top of the box. The children shouted out ideas such as blocks, books, puzzles, and basically anything they saw. They decided to try some books. Soon Fong was trying to balance a very large stack of books on top of a rounded handle of a basket that was on top of some plastic baskets that sat on a chair. The books were too heavy for Fong to hold, but the children were determined to reach the top. Books were falling all over the place, children were shouting, and I was afraid that I was losing control! We decided that using books was a good idea, but that it was not safe to continue. Fong and Xiaoming sat down with huge smiles on their faces, and I asked the children if anyone else had an idea.

Desmond suggested that we just stack books up by themselves, starting on the floor and going up to the top. When I asked him where we would stop, he clearly pointed to the top of the box. I restated his idea to the class, explaining that Desmond thought we should stack books from the floor all the way up. My finger stopped near the top, but not at the top. The children shouted that my finger was not at the top. I interpreted this as an understanding that the height of the box is from the floor to the top.

115

I was ready to end this line of discussion, though Ellen insisted that she also had an idea. She said to us, "We can take some tape and we can, like, make numbers on it. We can get some paper to write numbers on, and then we can, like, tape them, tape them together on the box and see how high the numbers are."

120

Although Ellen did have an interesting idea, at this point her classmates were clearly ready to move on. I informed the children that for Choice Time, one choice today would be to measure the box. Their eyes widened and, again, shouts of joy erupted! I was thrilled that there was so much interest in this and curious to see how they would go about the task.

125

C A S E   13

Measuring with nonstandard units

Rosemarie

GRADE 1, MAY

My first-grade class is working on a measurement unit. The children have compared two objects to determine which is longer. They have used their pencils as units of measurement to determine the lengths of books, strips of paper, blocks, and other objects in the classroom. They have also traced and cut out their own footprints and measured them using connecting cubes.

130

Today's lesson involved measuring lengths with their feet and hands. To start the lesson, I taped a 4-foot strip of masking tape on the carpet. With the children seated in a circle in the meeting area, I asked how we could measure the line on the floor.

135

Rosemarie

GEORGE: We could measure it with our hands or feet.

DANYA: Yeah! But our hands and feet are different sizes. Remember when we compared our footprints? Andrea's footprint is longer than mine is.

TEACHER: You say that we can measure this strip of tape with our feet. Can you predict how many of *my* feet it would take to measure the entire length of tape?

The predictions offered by the children were 4, 5, 6, and 7 foot-lengths. I started to walk along the strip, placing the heel of each foot directly against the toes of the one before. After two steps, I stopped and asked the children if they would like to change their predictions. The majority of the children then adjusted their predictions to 4 foot-lengths. I continued to walk to the end of the strip of tape, and we found that the tape was just slightly longer than 4 of my foot-lengths.

TEACHER: If I ask Asya to measure the strip with her foot-length, how many of her foot-lengths do you estimate it would take to measure the entire strip?

Many hands went up right away. Melanie estimated 7 foot-lengths, Lakshmi and Gita estimated 6 foot-lengths, and Tessa, Adriana, and Miriam estimated $7\frac{1}{2}$ of Asya's foot-lengths. Many of the children made very good estimates. In fact, it took $7\frac{1}{2}$ of Asya's foot-lengths to measure the entire strip.

I asked the children to work in pairs to measure different things in the room, using their hands and feet as the unit of measurement. They might measure the length of the bookshelf, the span of the doorway, each other's heights, and the length of the teacher's desk.

The children worked busily with their partners. I watched them as they measured, checking to make sure that they were beginning their measurements at the very end of the objects being measured, and that they were being careful about placing the heel of each foot directly against the toes of the other foot. Some children were lying on the floor so that their partners could measure their height in foot-lengths. Others were at the door, carefully balancing themselves as they made their way across the doorway, heel-to-toe. Still others were using their hands to measure the length of the windowsill.

Rosemarie

After some time, I asked the children to come back together in the meeting area with the information they had gathered.

TEACHER: How many of your foot-lengths does it take to measure the doorway?

As different children gave their measurements, I wrote them on a chart.

Miriam	12
Adriana	$10\frac{1}{2}$
Gita	10
Melanie	11
Kim	$10\frac{1}{2}$

TEACHER: By looking at this information, what can you tell me about the feet of these children?

COURTNEY: They're all pretty close in size. Maybe they all have the same size shoes.

CHANDRA: Miriam's foot is the biggest.

KJELD: No, Adriana's and Kim's feet are the biggest.

TEACHER: Take a minute to think about whose foot is the biggest. Keep that name in your head.

ISAAC: I know that Adriana and Kim used $10\frac{1}{2}$ foot-lengths, which means that they have the biggest feet.

COURTNEY: I just looked at the numbers, and Miriam has the highest number of foot-lengths, so I think her foot is the biggest.

MIRIAM: I think Gita has the biggest foot because it took fewer of her foot-lengths to measure the doorway. The smaller your foot is, the more feet you need to measure something.

TESSA: Why is it that when Gita and Adriana measured their footprints, their footprints were the same length, but when

175

180

185

190

195

they measured the doorway, they each ended up with a different number of foot-lengths?

VICTORIA: Adriana measured with her socks on, so she measured a little bit off because her socks made her feet bigger.

MELANIE: How were they walking? Were they walking heel-to-toe all the time?

TEACHER: That's a good point. You might want to try measuring again, being careful to start exactly at the edge of the length you are measuring, and making sure that your steps are precisely heel-to-toe, to see if you get the same measurement.

Initially I thought that the children knew that there was a relationship between the size of their feet and the number of steps necessary to measure the entire length of the strip of tape on the carpet. At the beginning of the lesson, they correctly predicted that Asya would have to use more foot-lengths than I would to measure the same strip of tape. However, when they were looking at the information on the chart, they were no longer sure of the relationship between the size of the foot and the number of foot-lengths. They thought that the higher the number of foot-lengths, the bigger the foot.

It wasn't until Miriam stated that the smaller the foot-length, the greater the number of foot-lengths required to measure a given length, that some of the children realized what the numbers on the chart indicated about the relative sizes of the children's feet. I'll follow this lesson with more exploration of this kind to make sure every child understands that different units of measurement yield different counts for the same length.

Walking to understand measuring

Dolores

PART ONE, NOVEMBER

At the end of October, my third graders had done some measuring with
rulers. In general, they seemed to have only limited experience with
rulers. I felt they also had a limited sense of distance. They didn't seem to
notice, or at least were not bothered by, other children getting very
different lengths when they all measured the same items.

It was early in the year and there was plenty of time to improve their
skills with measuring tools. I decided to shift my focus for a while, just to
help them develop a better sense of distance and the overall idea of
measuring. For the first activity, I assigned three fixed distances to be
measured using the children's actual feet. I decided to take advantage of
unusually wonderful November weather to do the measuring outside.
New lines had been painted on the blacktop play area, and I asked the
children to use their own feet as measuring tools to find the length and
width of the basketball court, as well as the length of any baseline of the
baseball diamond.

Twenty-one children set off with pencil and paper in hand to take these
measurements. Once we got back inside, we entered all their information
on a large chart (see Figure 15). I asked everyone to take just a few
minutes to look over the data and think about what was there. When they
seemed ready, I asked them what questions they had about the results. It
didn't take long for almost everyone to notice something to talk about.

"Karen has the smallest first number."

"Nate did the most steps on his first line."

"Two kids said the width is 62, but their other lines don't match at all."
As Chelsea said this, she pointed to Tyler's 108 and Crissy's 280 for the
basketball court length, and then their 60 and 47 for the baseline of the
baseball diamond.

225

230

235

240

245

Dolores

GRADE 3, NOVEMBER AND MAY

Student	Basketball court: length	Basketball court: width	Baseball diamond: length of baseline
Tyler	108	62	60
Karen	70	68	
Les	120 or 102	70	70
Curt	83	58	56
Omar	92	63	52
Nikki	117	$71\frac{3}{4}$	$67\frac{3}{4}$
Donald	97	59	56
Chelsea	117 + 2 in.	68 + 2 in.	67 + 5 in.
Dan	103	61	56 + 1 in.
Crissy	280	62	47
Nate	328 (102)	100 (65)	(76)
Chad	97	61	58
Beth	108	60	64
Francie	$113\frac{1}{2}$	69 + 1 in.	64
Cindy	76	60	69
Brandon	103	60	71
Kelli	102	61	58
Tommy	91	70	50
Cristal			
Felicity	109 + 6 in.	66	65
Henry	109	$64\frac{3}{4}$	60
Lily	126	52	

Parentheses ( ) indicate a measurement that was taken a second time.
Blank spaces indicate absences or incomplete work.

Figure 15 Results of measurements taken in "Kid-Feet" outside.

"Three of us said the width is 60, but look what happens on the other lines we measured." Henry was looking at Beth's, Cindy's, and Brandon's measures.

250

72   Measuring Space in One, Two, and Three Dimensions

"Yeah, someone's feet are shrinking, or growing."

"Shouldn't they be the same all the time?"

"Tyler and Henry have the baseline as 60, and their other numbers are close."

Many children noticed when others got results close to what they themselves reported.

We ran out of time, but it felt like there was the energy and interest to keep thinking about this. So the following day, I posted the chart where everyone could see it again. This time I asked the children to write in their math notebook anything they were confused by or found puzzling. I also asked them to write down anything they noticed this time that we hadn't seen before. Finally, they were to note any result they might want to double-check.

On this last issue, many children made note of Les's "120 or 102," Crissy's 280, and Nate's 328 as the basketball court length.

A few people wondered about Les and Tommy both getting exactly 70 on the width, but then 50 (Tommy) and 70 (Les) for the baseline.

Still others noticed three identical measurements of 56 for the diamond baseline (Dan added an inch, which was "a little more than my shoe"), with court width measurements that were all close (58, 59, and 61), but with court lengths that varied widely (83, 97, and 103).

A few students used the math notebook to confess "losing count" as they walked the lines to measure.

The children were really thinking about the results. Nate decided to do his count again because he thought he walked all the way around the basketball court.

In our earlier discussions, a few children had slipped in remarks about people getting the smaller numbers because they have larger feet. I was not sure everyone was able to grasp that idea, so several days later I wrote this on the board:

> Fred and George share a room. They each measured the room
> from the door to the window using their own feet, the way
> you did. Fred reported 30 steps, while George got 43 steps.
> How can that be?

Written responses included these:

"One might have lost count."

"One could have taken regular walking steps."

"One measured the room going the other way."

"Fred had larger feet."

"George had the bigger feet."

Clearly, different children had different understandings. For some, the confusion seemed to come from believing that *bigger numbers usually mean bigger* something else.

After many years of teaching third grade, I have come to expect the difficulties children experience with this concept. Usually, bigger and bigger go together: bigger hand and bigger mitten. Likewise, bigger foot, bigger shoe, bigger sock, bigger boot, and even bigger person seem to go together. Size is associated with clusters of things. There is something unsettling about measuring and finding that these connections do not hold true. Here, bigger foot means smaller count!

Devising the homework assignment was easy after I read all the children's thoughts about Fred and George. I asked them to do the following:

> Decide on a particular distance to measure at home, inside or outside. Teach an adult how we have been using the heel-to-toe measuring system. Record the steps it takes you and the number of steps it takes an adult to measure that distance.

In designing this assignment, I assumed that parents would have larger feet so the children would be faced with *larger feet means a smaller number*. The next morning, we collated the homework results into another chart (see Figure 16).

Again, after giving everyone a chance to look over these results, I asked the children to turn to their math notebooks to write down any questions that they had, or any interesting pieces of data they noticed. Almost every child noticed and wondered about the entry showing 17 steps for a student and $17\frac{1}{2}$ for the parent. (We were later to find out that this child hadn't actually done the homework, so she made up some numbers.)

Because all the other results had a larger number of kid steps and a smaller number of steps by the adults, it was easy for most children to say that smaller feet means you need to take more steps, and therefore you get a larger number.

Dolores

Kid steps	Adult steps		Kid steps	Adult steps
23	21		21	15
136	105		18	14
27	21		19	16
24	19		18	14
25	19		42	32
16	13		41	33
18	15		172	100
11	10		22	18
21	15		19	15
17	$17\frac{1}{2}$			

Figure 16 Heel-to-toe measurements of something at home.

Two results really got people's attention because they were so much larger than the others: 136 kid steps to 105 adult steps, and 172 kid steps to 100 adult steps. Upon further questioning, the class learned that both were measurements of distances outside, in the families' yards.

One pair of numbers, 11 kid/10 adult, drew attention both for the small number of steps and the closeness of the two numbers. Tommy, whose figures they were, explained that he and his mother measured the length of a sofa. He also confirmed what the class was predicting: that his feet were nearly as big as his mother's.

When we gathered back at the chart, I was amazed to listen as smaller conversations broke out about which children had feet close to the size of a parent's feet. The closest pairs of numbers—23/21, 19/16, 16/13, and 18/15—were pointed out. In their questions to one another, children tested their theory that in these cases, a child's foot would be pretty close to the parent's foot size.

The huge number, 172, didn't bother the class much because the child who reported those numbers was one of our smallest students, and he had his dad do the measuring with him.

Most of the class really seems to have grasped the idea of needing more of a smaller unit to measure a certain distance. They seemed to care more about the work because it involved using themselves as the measuring tools.

Dolores

It has been a foreign concept for my third graders to wonder about other people's ways to solve problems. I have been battling the idea that mathematics is just "write an answer and you're done." Now many children are getting the idea that it is a good thing to think over their own answers and other people's, too.

The children still need to become more familiar with rulers and develop something of an "inch sense" (not to mention the quarter inch, half inch, and so forth). I'm hoping all these topics will be easier for children if they are able to think out loud, allowing the rest of us to explore and discuss their ideas with them.

I hope these children are really on the way to feeling there is much more to mathematics than getting an answer.

PART TWO, MAY

Last fall when my class did some outdoor measurement on the playground, using their own feet as measuring tools, there was a concept that some students found quite tricky: that the larger the measuring unit, the smaller the number of those units it takes to measure a given distance, and likewise, the smaller the size of the unit, the larger the number of units. Through our activities, most of the class came to terms with this notion. However, because it can be such a slippery idea, I decided to check it out again nearly half a year later.

This time I gave children the task of measuring with handspans. They were to spread their fingers as wide as possible and use that hand-width as a tool to measure the length of our tables. The second task was to find the width of our hallway, using their actual feet with shoes on.

After they did the measuring, we put the data together into a table, just as we had done in the fall. To find out where each child stood with the ideas, I asked them to write answers to the following questions:

Who has the largest hand?
Who has the smallest hand?
Who has the largest foot?
Who has the smallest foot?
How can you be sure?

I was encouraged by what I read later that day. Most answered the first four questions correctly, although a few still had it backward.

Dolores

While the children were still writing, Les came up to me. After sitting for a long time, he now showed me that he had written nothing on his paper yet. He was really trying to think about the questions, but he couldn't see anything on the chart that would give him clues. It was clear to me that our earlier work measuring the playground was murky for Les, if not lost. To narrow the focus for him, we picked just two kids and the number of their handspans it took to measure the table. | 385

My attention was called away for half a minute but brought right back as Les called out, "You have to put your hand down more times if it is little!" A moment before, he had been in the dark; this idea had just come together for him. | 390

When we began class discussion the next day, Les couldn't wait to say what he knew: "Big hands and feet get low numbers and little hands and feet get high numbers because little things take up less room."

Chelsea added that people with big feet had to take fewer steps. Crissy | 395
announced that small hands needed to be put out more times to get to the end of the table. Cindy seemed to be confirming what she sort of thought was true when she said, "So big stuff takes up big room and the lowest number is a *big* thing?"

The conversation shifted to questions of accuracy. After a few minutes, | 400
I brought the group back together with another question: "When you look at the chart and see the biggest numbers, 15 and 18, doesn't that mean big hands?" I wanted to put the faulty thinking out on the floor so the students who had thought that way the day before would have some feedback from their peers without embarrassment. Classmates took this | 405
confusion seriously. They said things like, "You might think a big number means big hands or feet, but the big number means it is so small, you had to use it lots of times to get there." Someone even suggested that Henry hold up his big hand against Les's tiny hand.

I hope the discussion and demonstration helped everyone along, either | 410
by changing unsound ideas or by solidifying the sound ones.

Thinking about accuracy and precision

Mabel

I observed in Ms. Wilson's second grade on a day when they were starting
to revisit measurement of length. Earlier in the year, they had measured
strings and tapes that were as long as certain species of whale. Now
Ms. Wilson started the class by asking the children what they remembered
about measurement or rulers.

Bonnie said that if you only have two rulers and you want to measure
something really long, you could put the rulers down together. She
demonstrated putting down one ruler, then a second, then moving the
first to the place after the second, and so on. She then said that rulers were
good because if what you're measuring is too short, you can just take
away a ruler. If you were using a yardstick, you couldn't take it away.

Another girl argued that in fact you can measure something short with
a yardstick. To demonstrate, she and Bonnie tried using a ruler and a
yardstick to measure a strip of tape on the meeting area rug. They agreed
that you could measure it with either a ruler or a yardstick, but Alexis
said, "With a ruler you can take a ruler away, and with a yardstick, you
have to take away on it." I think she was imagining, for example,
something two feet long. If you put down three rulers, you could take one
of them away and see that the object was two feet long. With a yardstick,
you'd have to determine where on the yardstick the object ends and how
much you'd have to "take away" from the yardstick.

Nicole said that if you are measuring something long with one ruler,
you shouldn't put your finger down to mark your place before you move
the ruler because your finger takes up space and makes "it" (the "foot"
you measured with the ruler?) longer. Ms. Wilson reminded the class that
they had said that if you put your finger down between rulers once, it
might make just a little difference in your measurement; but if you used
your finger a lot of times, then it might make a big difference in your
measurement.

Mabel

Melody said that if you flip your ruler over itself to move it, then you don't make a space between the feet you're measuring.

Maya recalled that when they measured the whale lengths, different sets of partners got different measurements. Ms. Wilson confirmed this, and asked what the children thought of it. Melody said that she thought different pairs got different measurements because they used different methods of moving their rulers: flipping, using their fingers, or another way. She said even flipping makes a space between the rulers, and so nothing is perfect.

Melody's pronouncement of "nothing is perfect" struck a chord with the class and led the children to say "nobody's perfect" and the like. While the children seemed to relate to her statement on a personal level (or on the level of trite sayings, perhaps), I felt that Melody was expressing a mathematical thought. All the children who contributed at the meeting described issues involving measurement and accuracy, issues that had come up previously in the classroom. They seemed to be chewing on the fact that different methods of measurement are all imperfect and will lead to minor inaccuracies. I am not sure if they realized that there is, in a sense, both a "true" length and a "measured" length to objects, but this does seem to be an important part of the mathematics involved in measurement.

The discussion continued: Diana said that if you measured something shorter than a ruler, you could just put your finger on the ruler where the object ended. (She didn't say so, but reading that measurement can then be another interesting issue for second graders.) Ms. Wilson said that they would be looking for things to measure that were shorter than a ruler. She asked them to think about what to do when the thing they're measuring doesn't land exactly on a number on the ruler.

Immediately hands went up and children were talking about halves and quarters. Poonam explained that there is a little line in between each number line, and that if what you measured is closer to the middle line, you say it is $4\frac{1}{2}$ or $5\frac{1}{2}$. Maya asked whether it had to be exact or you should just decide if it's closer to the number or closer to the middle line. She also volunteered that she had a ruler at home with even more lines between the lines and you could measure more things with it. In my experience, children have always been interested in the "lots of little lines" on some rulers, but haven't really connected them to the kind of measuring that such a ruler could let you do. They didn't seem to relate the calibration to precision or accuracy of the measurement.

Mabel

It was very interesting to me that these children were so focused on the | 480
way you measured something and how that could affect the measurement
you obtained. This seems to be a very sophisticated issue for second
graders.

C A S E 16

Measuring: A different experience for everyone

Josie

Teachers of grades higher than mine often tell me that their students don't
know how to use a ruler to measure objects correctly, or that their | 485
students aren't able to estimate simple lengths. These comments made me
wonder why this is true. I teach my students how to measure and they are
able to do the task for me. Then I thought about the amount of time
during the school year that my students spend on this, and I realized that,
in my class, after learning to use a ruler, they really don't spend a lot of | 490
time measuring objects. I also thought about what I do myself that
involves measuring or using a ruler. Usually the only measuring I do is at
home. At school, I use a ruler primarily for making straight lines. This
thought made me realize that while all my students have rulers in their
desks, they also use them, mostly, to make straight lines; rarely do they | 495
use rulers for measuring. I decided that, given the comments from other
teachers, my students needed more ongoing experiences with measuring.

Consequently I designed an activity that requires each student to
measure one object in the class each week. Students were to record their
measurements on a chart on our math bulletin board. The only limitations | 500
were that they choose something that could be measured with the tools
available (we have rulers, yardsticks, metersticks, and tape measures), and
something that could be measured without climbing or otherwise risking

harm. I planned to choose three of the students' measurements from the chart each Monday and spend a little time discussing how the measurements were done, what tool was used, and how the measurer assured the accuracy of the measurement.

During the first week, every student found some time to complete this task. Having observed some of them measuring, I was pleased with most of what I saw, but had concerns about (1) some of their choices for a measurement tool, and (2) the accuracy of some of their measurements. Students who chose the tape measure had difficulty with its flexibility but didn't switch to a yardstick or ruler. One boy did not start his measurement at the end of the tape measure; it had a small metal tab at the end, and the student ignored this part and started his measurement after the tab. (In fact, he folded the tab back to get it out of the way.) At this point, I chose not to interfere or comment on the students' work. I would bring these issues up during discussion the following Monday, and I knew just which students' measurements to select for this.

Our follow-up discussion demonstrated more understanding than I had expected. Adam had measured the height of the file cabinet by using the tape measure. I selected Adam because I wanted to see if any other students would question his choice of the tape measure and how he used it. Adam demonstrated: He used a magnet on the file cabinet to hold the top end of the tape measure in place. He very carefully matched the top of the tape measure with the top of the cabinet and then just read the number on the tape measure that lined up with the bottom of the cabinet (the floor). No one questioned his use of the tape measure, so I asked him why he chose it. He answered, "It's longer than the meterstick, and I saw that it was longer than the file cabinet. I knew I would be able to measure the side with only one." The class discussed the benefit of this (not having to mark the end of a ruler or yardstick, then move it and measure more space). After our discussion, I no longer questioned his use of the tape measure.

Lisa was next. I chose her because she had measured the length of the chalkboard with a meterstick. She marked and labeled the end point of each length of the meterstick, then added the total of the four marked (numerical) measurements. Her procedure was clear and accurate. I wanted her to demonstrate what I had assessed as a successful technique. Of course, she made some errors when she demonstrated. She had originally made marks and labeled each 39 inches (she used the correct 39-inch line on the inch side of the meterstick). When she demonstrated her strategy for the class, she forgot this and made her marks at the end of the meterstick (approximately $39\frac{1}{4}$ inches). Her new total was then different from her original measurement. Presented with the two different numbers for the length of the chalkboard, Carla pointed out that Lisa's marks were not accurate "because of the little extra at the end of the meterstick." Carla and Lisa remeasured the chalkboard, correcting this error, and their new measurement agreed with Lisa's original one.

This led to a discussion about correct ways to use rulers, yardsticks, and metersticks. In the midst of this discussion, Robby explained, "You need to start at the zero."

TEACHER: Zero? I don't see a zero on any of these tools. What do you mean, zero?

ROBBY: The end of the ruler, before the 1, is zero.

TEACHER: If it's zero, why isn't there a zero? I've never seen a zero on a ruler.

ROBBY: Because there's no room to fit it. You're supposed to add an extra zero.

TEACHER: Who can explain this to me? Robby said you need to start at the zero. How can I start at the zero if it's not there?

MARCUS: They didn't put it there, but at the end of the ruler there is a zero.

TEACHER: [*pointing to the end with the 12*] At the end? Way down here?

MARCUS: No, the other end, the beginning.

TEACHER: So the end with the 1 is the beginning. Then why did Robby say we start with the zero? I still don't see a zero.

DEB: Because when you start at 1 on a tape measure or something, you should already have one inch.

RAUL: [*yelling out*] It's zero inches! You have to start at zero because that is where the inches start!

ROBBY: Yeah, the number 1 is at the end of one inch, not at the beginning.

TEACHER: What do other people think about this?

Other children agreed with Robby, Raul, Deb, and Marcus. 575

Next Marcus demonstrated his strategy to measure the width of the computer monitor with the tape measure. Marcus is the student I had observed folding back the metal tab, thus not starting at zero. When he demonstrated for the class, he did everything correctly. At some point he must have corrected himself or observed something that changed his 580 mind—he not only did it correctly, he also commented that he felt the tape measure was easier than the other tools, "because the computer is close to the wall and the yardstick would have been too long and wouldn't fit. I would need more than one ruler. And I could just fold the tape measure around the side of the monitor and read the number at the fold." 585

A lot more was discussed and a lot more happened during this math time. There were many ideas that we could have spent more time on. I'm sure some will come up again next week when we discuss the class's new measurements. I was amazed at the ideas (especially the zero conversation) that my students had. I had to admit that their ways—like Adam's 590 use of the tape measure—were not always what I would have done, and were not what I felt at first were the best ways, but they proved me wrong. There are many right ways.

This morning Adam had some time to do his new measurement. I noticed him at work when another student came over and asked if he 595 could get some tape for Adam, who needed it for his measurement. I supplied a piece of tape with no questions. I thought Adam would use the tape to mark the end of the meterstick, but when yet another student asked me for another piece of tape for Adam, I asked what he needed the tape for. I was told Adam was measuring the wall from the floor to the 600 ceiling. Recalling my original instructions (no measuring anything that would require climbing), I had to stop myself from saying, "He can't do that!" Instead, I took a closer look at what they were doing.

Adam was taping metersticks together, matching the end of one with the end of another to make one very long measuring stick. He had this 605 propped up against the wall in one corner of the room. He would add one meterstick, prop it up to check the height, take it down, tape on another meterstick, and repeat the procedure. Adam got as far as having a short length left at the top (shorter than a meterstick) when time was up and he had to stop. He has some thinking to do about how to measure this short 610 length. I know what I would do, but he'll probably think of something better, so I'll keep my mouth shut and let him work this out.

How far have we paced?

Sandra

GRADE 7, SEPTEMBER

My seventh-grade students, serious but smiling, stepped off from the starting point two by two. They carefully paced off the length of the sidewalk, from an imaginary line marking one corner of the school building to an imaginary line at the other end of the building. It was a beautiful day, and the students were glad to be measuring distances that could not be measured conveniently with a ruler. We were now working on a project to map the changes in the school grounds as official plans for building an addition got underway.

Earlier, we had measured a distance of 100 feet with a tape measure borrowed from the physical education department. Each student walked the distance eight times, taking normal steps, and recorded the number of paces on each trial. In the classroom afterward, students calculated their average feet per pace. At first they were amazed that their averages could be so different, but soon they agreed that some people take bigger steps than others.

When we returned to the classroom after carefully counting our paces along the sidewalk in front of the building, our goal was to calculate the distance in feet, using each student's average feet per pace. I expected there would be some discrepancies—measurements are always approximate—and I hoped the variety of answers would lead to a discussion about why the results were not all the same. I also thought that if that question got resolved, then we could explore mean, median, and mode of the data to see if these statistics would tell us anything about the distance. But we never got beyond the first question!

After the students had calculated the distance in feet, I listed their results, rounded to the nearest foot (see Figure 17). After everyone had a chance to look over the list, I asked for comments.

615

620

625

630

635

ANNIE: Most of the distances are between 100 and 120 feet.   640

NED: Bigger people had bigger numbers. For example, Lee had
              124 feet while Annie had 104.

JOCELYN: Wait a minute! Chuck had 85 and he's bigger than Lee and
              Annie, so how does that work?

DEIRDRE: We all had different feet per pace, so the answers had to be   645
              different.

Distance calculated to the nearest foot			
Molly	92	Olga	114
Wallace	108	Annie	104
Greg	116	Chuck	85
Joey	137	Indra	115
Jocelyn	114	Kate	117
Casey	110	Lee	124
Hayley	117	Serena	120
Deirdre	115	Constance	113
Masha	113	Andre	120
Ashraf	107		

Figure 17 Students' pace measurements translated to distance in standard feet.

There was some murmuring among pairs, so I let them discuss these
ideas with partners for a couple of minutes. As I listened in, I realized that
many students were fixed on the different averages as the cause of the
difference in results. They didn't understand that, once they converted   650
back to a standard unit of measure, their answers should be close to the
same. They seemed to think it was all right for one person to say the
distance was 85 feet while another said it was 124.

When I pulled the class back for a whole-group discussion, I asked five
different students this series of questions: 655

        Where did you start walking?
        Did you try to always keep walking at your normal pace?
        Where did you stop walking?

Not surprisingly, all the answers were the same. Some students looked very puzzled. Then one student, Annie, had an "aha!" moment. | 660

ANNIE: We all started at the same place and ended at the same place. Even though some of us take bigger or smaller steps, it shouldn't matter. We should all have the same result because we walked the same distance.

Most of the students didn't know what to make of Annie's statement. Unfortunately time was up, and they moved on to their next class. | 665

As I'm writing about it now, I realize Annie wasn't very clear in her statement, either. The issue is that they should all have the same result when calculated in feet—a standard unit. Many students were still tied to their belief that different-sized steps should give different answers for the | 670 distance. I realize now that we need to have a discussion of units—that across the class, a "pace" referred to different-sized units and so could yield different counts for the same distance, but a "foot" was consistent.

Now that I've had time to think through for myself what was stumping them, I'll need to figure out how to help them work on this | 675 issue. In the meantime, we all agreed to practice pacing on our own, and we would remeasure the distance across the front of the building at our next scheduled outdoor time.

C H A P T E R

4

Measuring area: Structuring rectangles

Many of the issues that arise with linear measure recur in the study of area: What is a unit? How is it applied? How do we think about parts of units? But area also brings its own challenges. First, a basic question: What is area? And then, What does it mean to measure it? What kind of units do we use? Does it differ from perimeter? To young children, these questions are quite complex. That was clear in Isabelle's case 3, where second graders were struggling to gauge the size of their meeting area, and it will again be apparent in Janine's case 18 and Lydia's case 21 in this chapter.

Understanding how the area of a rectangle is measured is basic to under-standing how the areas of many other shapes are measured, and here, too, there are complex ideas to be worked through. Children learn to say "area equals length times width," but may not understand the units to which this equation refers, why multiplying linear dimensions yields a count of units of area, or even that the equation applies only to rectangles.

An important step in understanding the area of a rectangle is visualizing it as an array of squares, an arrangement of equal rows and equal columns, like this 3×4 rectangular array of squares.

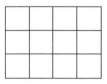

Georgia's case 19 and Maura's case 20 show us children working with arrays. Beyond seeing the individual squares, they must also recognize rows composed of those squares, columns composed of those same squares, and how multiplication yields the count of squares.

In this chapter, we see third and fourth graders working on all of these issues. As you read, consider these questions:

■ In cases 18–20, which issues involved in the measure of rectangles are the children working on?

■ In case 21, when children are challenged to measure the odd shape of their hands and feet, what new issues arise?

C A S E   **18**

Getting around the issues of space

Janine

GRADE 4, JANUARY

I recently finished a unit on three-dimensional geometry and was now interested in the students' understanding of one- and two-dimensional space. That is, I wanted to hear what they had to say about area and perimeter. The first day, I decided to work with only four students so I could really concentrate on their issues.

5

Janine

First I asked what they understood about one dimension. They said that it was a measurement of height or width, and they described it as a line. They drew several lines of different lengths and told me that they would use a ruler to measure how long things were—like the door or the floor or their height. I asked how they would measure items that were larger and they told me they could use a yardstick or a meterstick, and that they would use a mile measure to show the size of really big things, like the distance across our city. I was satisfied with their understanding of one-dimensional measures—at least as far as I wanted to go just now.

We moved on to two dimensions. They said that the two dimensions were height and width, like a rectangle. It's tall and it's wide. Examples they gave as they looked around the room were the door, the table, the windows, their paper. Although the door had some depth, "if we were just looking at the front face, it would be 2-D."

We had some color tiles, so I asked them to make a rectangle and talk about how big it was. They took 8 tiles and made a 4×2 rectangle. I asked them about the size of the rectangle; they said it was 8, and that around the edges was 12. I questioned them about these numbers: 8 what? 12 what?

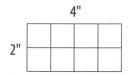

We have done some work with the array model of multiplication, in which a 4×2 rectangle was translated as 8. But now I was asking a different question; I was asking about the size of the rectangle, and the numbers 8 and 12 without units attached said nothing about size. After some thought, the children were able to tell me that the 12 meant 12 inches around. (The color tiles are one-inch squares, so the rectangle was 12 inches around). I then asked what the 8 meant.

JULIO: 8 squares?

SADIE: Right, the rectangle is 8 squares big.

TEACHER: What if the squares were a different size? The rectangle would be larger or smaller, but you could still say it has 8 squares. Is there some way to describe exactly how big this particular rectangle is?

JUAN: Yes. It's 8 square inches. Each of the tiles is 1 square inch, so the whole thing would be 8 square inches. That would be the size of this rectangle.

We took a few minutes to review a square inch, a square foot, and so forth. Everyone seemed OK with this, but I wasn't sure how much they really understood.

Now I asked the group to take some paper and rulers and draw a rectangle that was 8 square inches in size (4×2 inches or 1×8 inches). They immediately took the tiles and began to trace them, so I asked them not to use the tiles, but to think about it another way. Everyone was eventually able to do this with rulers, but only after lots of discussion. They also drew a rectangle that was 1×5 inches and were able to tell me that the perimeter of this rectangle was 12 inches, and the "inside space" was 5 square inches. That "inside space," that "bigness," was what I was really interested in having them look at.

I happened to see a piece of heavy cardboard on the radiator, so I brought it over to the table and asked the children to figure out how big the cardboard was. (Its measurements were 18×12 inches.) They immediately started laying the color tiles on the cardboard, in a line along the inside of each edge. I had hoped they would use their rulers.

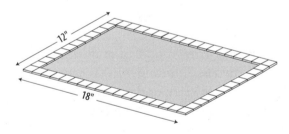

Figure 18 The children laid tiles inside the edges of a piece of cardboard to determine its size.

JUAN: The dimensions are 18×12. The area is 56. I know the area is 56 because I counted all the squares around.

SADIE: $18 + 18 = 36$; $12 + 12 = 24$. That's 60! It's not 56, Juan.

JUAN: It's $10 + 10$, not $12 + 12$.

I really wanted this conversation to continue, because I've seen students confused about this same question before. What do you count when you're counting area, and what do you count for perimeter?

JULIO:	No. It's 12 + 12. There's twelve on each side.	
JUAN:	But you're counting the corners twice when you do it that way.	65
SADIE:	Huh?	
JUAN:	[*pointing to the four corners*] When you add 12 + 12 and 18 + 18, you're counting the corners two times. You have to take the four corners away.	70
NOEMI:	No, you have to take two away. Are you talking about these two corners [*pointing to the top two*]?	
JUAN:	No, all four corners. See, if you do 18 + 18, you already counted the four corners. Then when you do the sides, you have to count 10 + 10.	75
JULIO:	[*nodding*] Right, we were counting the corners twice.	

Juan very carefully explained about the corners again, sketching a diagram similar to Figure 19.

| JUAN: | If you count the two 18s, you have to take the four corners out because they are part of the 18. | 80 |

Juan was pretty good at explaining himself. Everyone now agreed that the number of squares inside the edge, which they were calling the *area*, was 56. I tried to steer them to think about what area is.

| TEACHER: | So the area is 56? How did you figure out the area for your 4 x 2 rectangle? | 85 |
| JUAN: | We multiplied 4 times 2 and got the area. | |

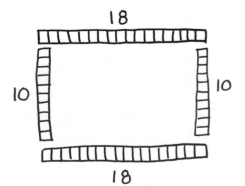

Figure 19 Juan drew a diagram like this in his effort to show that you shouldn't count the corners twice when you figure perimeter.

TEACHER:	So what's the area of this rectangle?
JULIO:	Oh, boy, now I'm totally confused. The 56 is the perimeter, not the area, isn't it?

A chorus of "area," "perimeter," "area," "perimeter," echoed around the group.

NOEMI:	Wait a minute. The 56 is the "around," isn't it? The "around" is the peri... peri....
SADIE:	Yeah. It's the outside, not the inside.
NOEMI:	You don't have 56 on the inside [*pointing to the part of the cardboard that was not covered by the colored tiles*]. Do you see 56 blocks on the inside?

I knew they were confused about how to measure the perimeter, but I wanted to listen to their ideas and not correct them at this point. Later I would help them see that the perimeter is 60 inches, not 56. For now, they needed to think about area.

JULIO:	No—but if we cover the entire cardboard with squares, we can figure out what the area is.
JUAN:	It's 18 times 12. If you know 18 times 12, you know the area.

Noemi started to multiply 18 times 12 and was complaining about how hard it was.

TEACHER:	Do you think Juan is right? Do you think if you multiply 18 times 12, you will get the area?
JUAN:	It is, because there are 18 squares going across and there are 12 rows going down. That's twelve 18s—18×12 will give you the area.
JULIO:	[*proudly*] I know what it is. It's easy. I broke up the 12 into 10 and 2: 18 times 10 is 180, 18 times 2 is 36, 180 plus 36 is 216.

The group now had a brief discussion about breaking apart numbers to facilitate multiplication. We had been working on that for the last few days. I saw that in one case, at least, it had sunk in!

Janine

GRADE 4, JANUARY

TEACHER:	So do you all agree that the area is 216? [*Everyone is in agreement.*] So how big is the cardboard?
JUAN:	The perimeter is 56 *inches.*
JULIO:	And the area is 216 tiles. No, *square inches:* 216 *square inches!*

120

I think that the concept of area as the measure of the inside space or surface space is really, really hard for my students. Up to this point, my class has been looking at the shapes of geometric figures in these terms: how many sides? how many angles? faces? vertices? They have considered whether a shape is a rectangle, a square, a hexagon, or even a cube. They have been describing the shapes. Now, with area, they need to look at the size of the space enclosed within the shape, the measure of that space. And they need to measure in squares: square inches, square feet, square centimeters, and so forth.

How do students think about the sizes of two-dimensional objects in daily life? Do they see the size as the perimeter? Is the size of a desktop how big around it is? Do they ever think about the area of the desk's surface?

I was really curious about how they would see and describe the size of a box, or the size of their classroom. They seemed to have some understanding that one dimension is a line, that two dimensions have height and width, and that three dimensions include depth (or "deepness," as they often call it). But for those last two dimensions, do they understand that "the space inside" is an important measure of size? Do they think about volume at all?

Perimeter, on the other hand, seemed easier, but I see that they are still confused about that, too. I thought their logic was OK until I really listened to and thought about what they were doing. I became so intrigued with the four-corners discussion that I almost lost track of the fact that they were measuring the perimeter incorrectly. Where did they get confused? They seemed to understand perimeter when we were talking about smaller rectangles (4×2) and (1×5). Was it their technique—trying to measure the dimensions of the cardboard with the tiles—that threw them off? What if they had used a ruler? Would they have come up with the same perimeter? Would they have been able to think about the perimeter more clearly?

I also need to go back and think about the area model for multiplication to see if there is a way that I can connect this to geometric area. We

may call it the "area model" for multiplication, but that doesn't neces- | 155
sarily mean that students understand the "area" part. They do seem to
recognize that a 2×4 array means 2 groups of 4 (or 4 groups of 2), but
there is something about the "area-ness" that I need to think more about.

The session ended before we could get back to the perimeter problem.
I think it would be a good problem to present to the whole class. I'm
willing to bet that others in the class will find it equally challenging. | 160

Even though the matter of perimeter was unresolved by the end of the
session, discussions like this one are really helpful in pinpointing some of
those sticky points in student understanding. I find that working with a
small group sometimes highlights issues that are likely to come up later in
the larger group, issues that I may want to watch for more closely. When I | 165
start working with the whole class, many more issues will come up, I'm
sure, but at least some of them won't be such a surprise!

C A S E   **19**

A big clump of cake

Georgia
GRADE 3, NOVEMBER

Our third-grade class has been studying multiplication for about three
weeks. Children have read picture books that contain equal groups of
objects, written word problems, skip counted and looked for patterns on | 170
hundred charts, and constructed arrays with square tiles.

As a diagnostic tool, I asked the class to draw three arrays:
one 3×4, one 5×4, and one array that makes a square. The children's
drawings showed me the different ways they were seeing the structure of
an array (see Figure 20). For example, in his first two arrays, Diego drew | 175
rows, but his squares were not aligned in columns. Cynthia drew in each
square, one by one. And Savanna drew straight lines through her
rectangle to mark off rows and columns.

	Draw a 3 × 4 array.	Draw a 5 × 4 array.	Draw an array that makes a square.
Diego			
Cynthia			
Savannah			

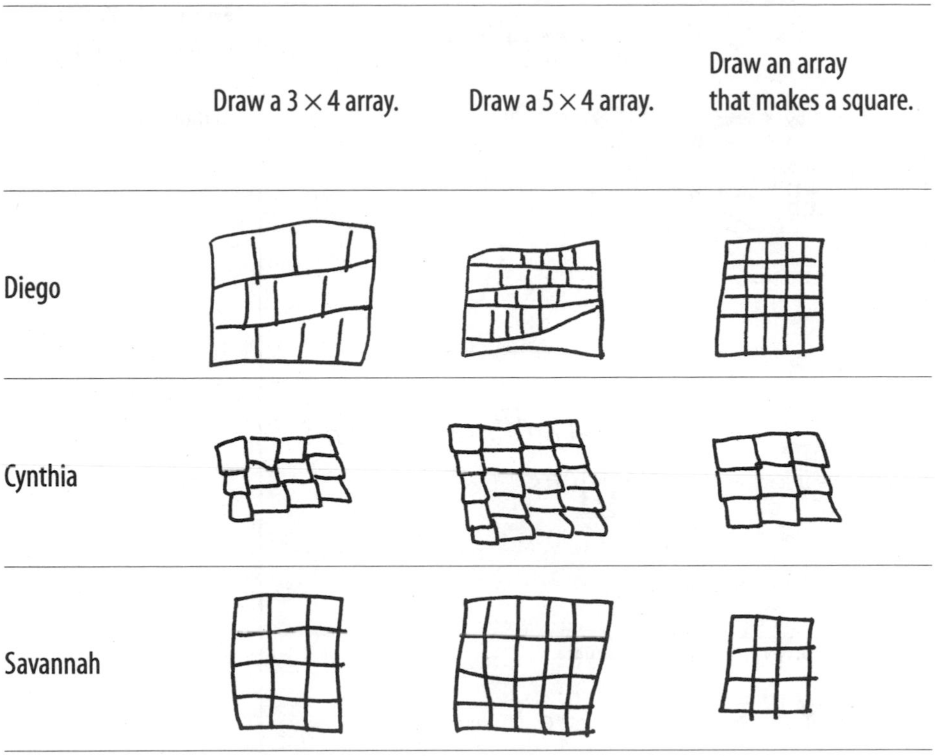

Figure 20 Diego, Cynthia, and Savannah had different ways of seeing an array.

Figure 21 shows the work of Kalil, a child who has seemed particularly confused by the concept of multiplication. Outside of school, he has been drilled on his multiplication facts and can quickly tell you a memorized answer to a multiplication problem. I have had the sense, however, that he really didn't understand what he was doing. On his paper he wrote, "I don't get this."

What follows is an account of my meetings with Kalil, one-on-one, over the next two days, as I tried to understand his thinking about multiplication and about arrays.

DAY ONE

I begin our meeting by asking Kalil what he "doesn't get" when he's asked to draw a 5 × 4 array. He replies, "I don't get this because 5 and 4 won't go. I messed up and I got to 26."

Name __Kalil__
Date __11/16__

Draw a 3 by 4 array.

_____

Draw a 5 by 4 array.

I don't get this one

_____

Draw an array that makes a square.

I don't realy get this one

Figure 21 Kalil is confused by arrays and their connection to multiplication.

I ask him to try it again so I can watch what he is doing. Starting in the left hand corner, he carefully draws what are meant to be squares, one at a time. He draws a row of 4 going across the top. Then he draws 5 down the right side, not counting the corner square as one of his 5 (drawing at left).

195

Then he goes back to fill in each row and gets stuck. He knows he needs to have 4 squares in each row, but he doesn't count the column he initially drew on the right as part of his array. What he actually draws is a 4×5 array inside the frame he originally drew (see drawing above, right).

When he starts to count the squares, he begins to count all of them, including the frame, but soon stops, saying, "I can't really count this."   200

TEACHER: What do you mean?

KALIL: I counted to 24. That's when I stopped. I couldn't really count it, it's so messy.

TEACHER: Why did you start by drawing this? [*I point to what I'm calling the frame.*]   205

KALIL: I knew that if I started like that, I'd continue drawing fours until I got to the bottom.

At this point I'm wondering if there's something about keeping track of these squares as he draws that's throwing him. I want to figure out   210
whether it's the concept of arrays or the task of drawing arrays that's stumping him.

I pull out the square tiles and ask Kalil to make a 5 × 4 array. He again starts by arranging a line of 4 tiles along the top and another 5 tiles down the right side, without counting the corner in common. He then adds tiles   215
to make rows of 4, one row at a time, until it looks like this:

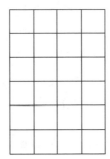

"OK," I think, "This definitely isn't a drawing problem."

TEACHER: What does a 4 × 5 array mean to you?

KALIL: Four of the fives.

TEACHER: What does that mean?   220

KALIL: I don't really know what that means.

TEACHER: What about 4 times 5? What does that mean to you?

KALIL: It means that I'm doing groups and I multiply them.

TEACHER:	Where are your groups in this array?
KALIL:	I don't know. You said multiplication takes you into groups and you plus them.
TEACHER:	Do you know what that means?
KALIL:	Not really. In other words, no.

I decide to abandon arrays altogether for now. The arrays seem to be confusing him. He doesn't see the groups within the rows or the columns. We need to go back to the concept of multiplication as equal groups in a way that will work better for him.

TEACHER:	Use the tiles to show me 2 groups of 3, but make it really clear that it's 2 separate groups.

Kalil builds a 4 × 4 array. He's going backward, not forward!

TEACHER:	Where are the 2 groups of 3?
KALIL:	Here's 2, here's 2, here's 3. [*He points to the array as shown.*]

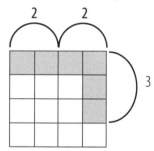

At this point, my heart is sinking. It seems that he's just grabbing at straws, pointing at the numbers he hears without thinking about what they mean. He's probably reading my face because when I ask him what array he has built, he says with chagrin, "Oh yeah, that's a 3 x 4."

I ask him to try it again. "Show me 2 groups of 3," I repeat. Kalil builds something that looks like this:

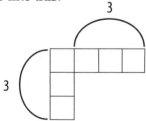

He points out the threes making up the two legs. I need to get him away from arrays! So I try a new tack: "Instead of making it in an array, make piles. Make 2 piles of 3." | 245

Kalil stacks 3 tiles, then 2, then 3, then 2, then 3 again, happily exclaiming, "I'm making a pattern! 2, 3, 2, 3..."

I'm feeling frustrated at not finding a way to help Kalil connect with the ideas. At this point, I'm ready to quit teaching and find a job flipping hamburgers. | 250

TEACHER: Kalil, make 2 groups of 3.

KALIL: Oh, yeah, 2 groups.

He stacks 3 tiles and then stacks another 3 tiles. It's interesting to me that he chooses to stack the tiles because they are not easily stacked. | 255

He finally has something that could be considered a right answer. But it's so tenuous, and so teacher-led. As long as he stays away from arrays for a while!

TEACHER: Now make 5 groups of 3. [*Kalil starts making stacks of 5.*] Five groups.... [*He redirects himself and builds 5 stacks of 3.*] | 260

We do a few more of these until I'm convinced that he can understand the language of equal groups. Several times, I ask him, "How many groups do you have? How many are in each group?" and he's able to respond correctly. But this doesn't necessarily connect to multiplication for him, as I find out with my next question. | 265

TEACHER: Show me 4 times 3. [*Kalil immediately starts building a faulty array.*] No, show me 4 groups of 3.

He starts stacking equal groups. What he needs is to make the transition between these equal groups and multiplication.

TEACHER: OK, so now you have 4 times 3. Show me 2 times 6. | 270

He does make this transition, at least with me sitting right there with him. We do several more examples. He's able to build stacking models that correspond with the multiplication problems.

But I'm still thinking about this problem with arrays. Arrays are a big part of the math curriculum, so I feel that he needs to understand them, too. I decide to see if maybe he can make this next transition as well.

275

TEACHER: Now show me 3 groups of 2, but instead of building them in stacks, lay them flat.

Without hesitating, Kalil makes a 3 × 2 array out of tiles.

TEACHER: Can you separate them a little to show 3 groups of 2? [*He does.*]

280

TEACHER: [*pushing the tiles back together into the array*] Now show me 2 groups of 3.

KALIL: You can't. Look.

285

He pushes apart the tiles to make two groups, but they clearly don't have three tiles in them.

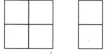

He's finally beginning to see this array as having groups that form the columns, but he's not seeing that the rows are also in groups. I decide to show him.

290

TEACHER: What about like this?

KALIL: Oh! It's like a big cake. You take a knife and chop it in two.

We do a few more of these and then quit for the day. I'm aware that I've done a lot of different things with him in one day— perhaps too many, too fast—and I'm not quite sure what will stay with him. I decide to meet with him again the next day.

295

DAY TWO

The next day, I start by saying, "Let's go back to some of the things we were working on yesterday. Would you please build a 4 × 3 array?"

Kalil starts to make stacks of tiles, then lays them flat to form the edges of an array, then switches back to stacks. "I'm going to do it in piles," he announces. As he builds, he says aloud to himself, "three groups of four." He makes 3 stacks of 4 tiles each.

300

TEACHER: If you wanted to take these piles and turn them into an array, how would you do that?

Instead of taking the 12 tiles he was already working with, Kalil pushes them away and takes out new tiles to build the following:

305

TEACHER: What do you have there?

KALIL: A 3 × 3.

TEACHER: You want a 3 × 4.

He builds a 3 × 4 array.

310

TEACHER: How do you know you have a 3 × 4?

Kalil shows me the 4 along the top and the 3 along the side. This time, for the first time, he is counting the corner tile as part of the 3 and as part of the 4.

TEACHER: Can you show me 3 groups of 4?

Kalil separates the array in columns, making 4 groups of 3.

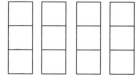

He looks at it, pushes it back together, and repeats it again, two or three times. It is clear to me that he knows he has 4 groups of 3, not 3 groups of 4, but he can't figure out what else to do. Finally, as if a light-bulb has gone on, he separates the array by rows, finally identifying the 3 groups of 4.

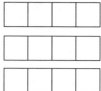

I am curious about one last thing: whether drawing an array requires different understandings and skills than building it. So I ask Kalil to draw the 3 × 4 array he has just built. He draws it perfectly.

TEACHER: Where are the groups of 3 in your drawing?

Kalil takes his pen and draws a line straight through each column.

TEACHER: Where are the groups of 4 in your drawing?

He draws lines through every row, remarking, "What reminds me of it is, this is a big clump of cake. My knife will cut it, like this."

I am left with questions about what happened with Kalil and what will happen next. What will he retain of these understandings over time? Is the array model so confusing for him that I should have abandoned it? What role did his visualization of a cake and a knife have in helping him see the rows and columns in arrays? Does drawing an array require different understandings and skills than building one? How significant is it that he draws arrays one square at a time?

330

335

C A S E   20

How do third graders measure area?

Maura

GRADE 3, MAY

Last week I set up an activity in my classroom for the express purpose of finding out what my third graders already understood about the concept of area. If I asked them to compare two spaces that seemed close in area, how would they go about measuring the two areas to solve the problem? I decided to create this situation primarily because it was getting late in the year, and although we had done several investigations into linear measurement, I didn't feel that we had adequately addressed other kinds of measurement. I wanted to treat the concept of area explicitly, even though earlier in the year my students did a fair amount of work with

340

345

arrays during their multiplication unit. I felt it was important that they experience area as a measurement and consider real-life situations in which they would need to measure space rather than just distance. I suspected that they had had very little experience with this in earlier grades, and I was curious about how they would approach it.

The problem that I gave my third graders involved designing an imaginary garden. I told them that I wanted to dig a garden but couldn't decide what shape I wanted it to be. I showed them diagrams of the two shapes I was considering (see Figure 22).

I told students that I wanted to figure out whether these two gardens would each give me the same amount of planting space, or if one had more space than the other. Since I wanted to have as much planting space as possible, the answer would determine which shape I would choose for the garden. I asked the children to figure out the answer for me, and also asked how they might go about doing this.

LEAH: Make squares that are 6 inches and 5 inches, and cover them up.

JEREMIAH: Take one away from the 7 and give it to the 5, to make 6, and then it's the same.

LIAM: Just multiply.

DYLAN: I don't have to do this. I already know this. They're the same.

I accepted all possibilities, writing them on the board, but didn't comment on any—except to tell Dylan that he had to prove it to me. Then I sent them off to work in pairs, giving each pair copies of the two shapes. The garden plots were each drawn on a separate sheet of paper, with a

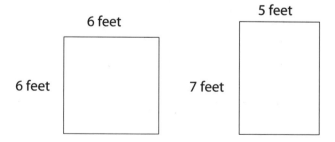

Figure 22 Two proposed garden shapes, presented as an area problem.

scale of 1 inch to 1 foot. (I made no indication of the scale on their papers, however; I simply labeled the dimensions as "feet.") I also pointed out a variety of materials on the table that they could use if they wanted—rulers, yardsticks, interlocking cubes, square tiles, scissors, blank paper, and 1-inch square graph paper. I offered no suggestions of what to do with any of these things. I was wondering if anyone would actually measure the "gardens" out on the floor with the yardsticks, but no one did.

As children started to work, I went to talk to Dylan, who was still insisting that he didn't need to do anything. Dylan was without a partner, because we have an odd number in the class and he sometimes works best alone. I asked him to tell me why he thought the two gardens were the same. He added the 7 and 5 to get 12, and explained that because 6 and 6 was also 12, then they had to be the same.

TEACHER:	You've told me that the numbers add up to the same thing, but how does that tell me that the space is the same in both gardens?
DYLAN:	Here, I'll show you.

Dylan put the paper with the rectangle garden on top of the paper with the square garden. The paper was transparent enough for us to see the lines underneath, and he matched up both shapes along the bottom left corner. He pointed to the "extra" along the side of the square, and measured it with his thumb and index finger.

DYLAN:	See, this part [*the "extra" at the right*] is about the same as this part [*the "extra" at the top*].

He moved his thumb and finger up to the extra piece of the rectangle, across the top of the square, and with only a small adjustment, discovered that he could make it match!

DYLAN:	Well, it's *really* close.
TEACHER:	But Dylan, how can you find out if those two extra pieces are *exactly* the same size?

Maura

GRADE 3, MAY

DYLAN: OK, I've got an idea.

He went off to get something—scissors, as it turned out—while I checked in with Leah and Janis. They were arguing.

LEAH: But Janis, you don't have to do that! All you have to do is put the tiles along the edges!

JANIS: I want to do it this way!

Janis was filling in the rectangle with square tiles. Leah was trying to get her to stop.

TEACHER: What's up, girls?

LEAH: Janis says you have to fill the whole thing in, but I think all you have to do is cover the edges, and then add them all up.

TEACHER: So why don't you each do it the way that you want to, and then explain to the other what you did? Leah, you can show me what you mean on the square while Janis finishes the rectangle.

Leah laid tiles down along the top and the left side of the square.

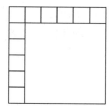

TEACHER: So how will you count these?

LEAH: There's 6 along the top, and 6 down the side, so that means it's 6 sixes, and that's… [*she thinks for a moment*] 36.

Teacher: You're saying that these tiles on the side are… what?

LEAH: That's where the next row is. You can just fill them in. [*Leah starts to fill them in, and then looks over at Janis's work.*] Oh, it's the same thing, isn't it?

TEACHER: Janis, what did you come up with?

      Measuring Space in One, Two, and Three Dimensions

JANIS: This one's smaller, because it's only 35.   425

At this point, I would have asked them to try Leah's strategy on Janis's rectangle, but Dylan was back.

DYLAN: Teacher, look. I cut them out, but this piece is bigger than this one.

Dylan had cut out both shapes and laid them on top of each other   430 again. He had also cut the "extra" off the right side of the square, but left the extra piece of the rectangle sticking out above the square. He took the cut-away strip and laid it across the top of the square to show me that it was indeed longer than the top of the rectangle.

TEACHER: So which shape is bigger, the rectangle or the square?   435

DYLAN: The square, because its extra piece is bigger.

I asked him to go write down what he did. Then I moved on to see what others had done. I found variations on a couple of themes, all around the room. Children quickly discovered that the square tiles are a useful material, and several were covering their shapes much the way   440 Janis did. No one had chosen the interlocking cubes, which, being $\frac{3}{4}$-inch cubes, would present an interesting challenge. I heard the words "square inch" in a few places, referring to the tiles, but unfortunately didn't get a chance to find out how that term emerged—did someone measure the tiles? No one seemed surprised that the tiles fit so neatly into   445 the space labeled "6 feet"—and exactly six of them at that! Should I have been surprised that these third graders internalized the idea of scale so effortlessly? Or did I just make it too obvious?

I also saw rulers being used. Cody and Jeremy had cut out their shapes and laid them on top of each other, the same way Dylan did. Instead of   450 cutting away the extra to see if one "extra" matched the other, they measured both lengths with a ruler. Cody reported that the square had 6 inches, but the rectangle only had 5, so the square was bigger.

Maura

GRADE 3, MAY

Liam used his ruler in a very different way. He drew lines across each of his shapes at one-inch intervals. In the spaces, he wrote numbers that represent skip-counting.

455

6
12
18
24
30
36

5
10
15
20
25
30
35

Liam was another child, like Dylan, who started out saying that he already knew the solution, and that both shapes were the same size. I don't know how he moved from his addition model to this solution that clearly involved multiplication, but now he seemed to have a very clear sense of the rows, and how many square inches (or was he thinking square feet?) each row represented. I had wondered if anyone would hearken back to the arrays we had worked with before, but no one used that term. The connection, however, seemed to be here anyway.

460

We did two more days of area activities, involving both measuring and comparing areas of different size and shape. I was impressed with how quickly the idea of covering the space with a standard measure—the tiles—became a fixture in their work. I was also struck by how many students were able to use what they knew about linear measurement and incorporate it into work with area. By the end of the week, we were even quite close to the standard formula for area of a rectangle (length times width), since many students were using a multiplication model. My next question is: Will they hold onto this until they revisit it in a later grade?

465

470

Up in arms over hands and feet!

Lydia

GRADE 3, FEBRUARY

If you have ever tried to retrieve a word that's on the tip of your tongue, you know how frustrating it can be. That feeling is a good metaphor for the frustration I am currently feeling about the math activity I'm about to describe. There is a big idea playing itself out repeatedly in my class's investigations of area, but I get only fleeting glimpses of it and can't seem to get my mind around it. Let me explain. | 475

In previous investigations of area, my students have worked solely with rectilinear shapes (shapes bounded by straight lines). For this kind of problem, I have noticed that many children chose to measure certain shapes by covering them with objects of the same shape. For example, they used the red trapezoid from the pattern blocks when they were asked to determine the area of a table with a trapezoidal shape. Another time I asked them to figure out the area of our square meeting rug; many children chose to cover the rug with the square hundreds flats from the set of base ten blocks. Considering the children's comments and actions, I was left wondering the following: | 480

| 485

■ Given an irregular shape for which there are no matching manipulatives, what would the children use as a measuring tool? Would they default to square units, or try to find a better "fit"? | 490

■ If they do decide to use square units to measure the area of an irregular shape, will they see the units as something that can be broken into smaller parts, to accommodate the irregular areas that don't divide neatly into squares? Or will they view the units as square shapes that need to remain intact? | 495

■ Many children now understand that the area of a rectangle can be represented as the length times the width. When the shape being measured does not have straight sides, will the children still try to use linear measurement to figure out the area? | 500

In previous years, I had used a math activity from *A Collection of Math Lessons* in which students measure the area of their foot on graph paper.* I now decided to modify this activity in a way that would let me investigate how children come to understand area.

I told the class that I wanted them to think about how they could figure out the area of one of their hands or feet. Some students decided to measure the area of their hands; others chose feet. I asked them to take a minute to think about what they might use to solve this problem. I told them I would provide anything they needed that they couldn't find in the room, but I was reluctant to lead them toward any one tool.

Libby looked pensive and asked, "Is the area of your foot your shoe size?"

This question elicited a flurry of comments, most in assent. A moment later, a few children got up and retrieved measuring tapes from the math bin. Many others soon followed suit. They began to measure the length or width or perimeter of their hand or foot. Those measuring their feet noticed that these dimensions did not reflect their shoe size. They also quickly realized that there was no single "length" or "width"; each dimension varied a lot, depending on what part of their foot they measured.

EDWARD: This is hard. The rug we measured had straight sides, but your feet are wavy. My foot is three and a half inches wide here [*points to his heel*] but only two inches here [*points to instep*].

One child took the tape measure and tried to wrap it around his hand repeatedly to form a makeshift glove. Some children were writing their many measurements in their math journals and adding up the numbers. Ben wrapped the tape measure around the outside of his sneaker.

BEN: Mine is 24.

EDWARD: No, that's the perimeter.

BEN: Oh yeah.

---

* From M. Burns, *A Collection of Math Lessons from Grades 3 through 6* (White Plains, NY: Cuisenaire, 1987).

Measuring Space in One, Two, and Three Dimensions

One thing was becoming clear: When given a nonrectilinear shape, many of the children were unclear about the difference between linear and area measurement. These same children seemed to clearly differentiate between linear and area measurement when they successfully figured out the area of our square rug. What was happening? I didn't know where this was leading or what I'd do next. Only a few students asked for graph paper or made any attempt to trace their hand or foot on paper. 535

One child retrieved the bin of color cubes and began to place cubes on his hand, but he abandoned the idea when they didn't fit perfectly and started to tumble off his fingers. This boy's actions were intriguing enough, however, to get some of the other children interested in finding something that they could use to cover their hands. They tried color tiles and unit centimeter cubes, but soon abandoned these, too, when they kept falling off. It was interesting that the children chose only square-shaped manipulatives as measuring tools. Although I can't point to the activity or discussion that might have been the turning point, it seemed that the children who understood the difference between perimeter and area knew, too, that area is conventionally measured in square units. 540 545 550

At this point, Emma started to trace her hand onto a notebook page in her journal. Soon everyone was tracing a foot or hand onto a page in their journals. Many of the children again reverted to measuring the various dimensions of their tracings with the tape measure—length of each finger, width of the hand across the palm, width across the fingers—and recording these dimensions on their tracings. Then they added up the measurements and recorded their totals (see Figure 23). It didn't seem to bother them that some lengths went unmeasured. 555

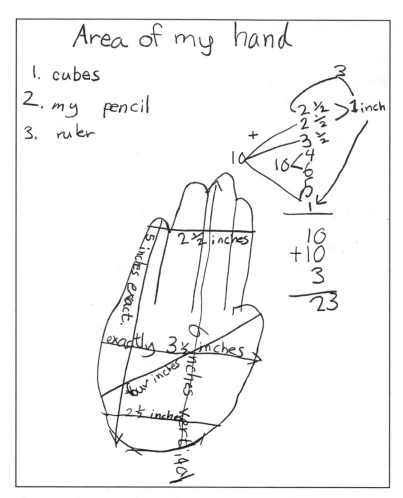

Figure 23 This girl's approach was typical of many; she measured a lot of different linear dimensions and tried adding them up.

The five or so children who requested graph paper at the start of the activity were busily counting the squares inside their hand and foot tracings. The children who seemed to know how to solve the problem almost immediately were also able to deal with the partial squares inscribed in their tracings. They matched the partial squares with other partial squares that together would form a square unit (see Figure 24). These students seemed to possess a deeper understanding of a square unit as a unit of measure that they can take apart and recombine without its losing meaning.

560

565

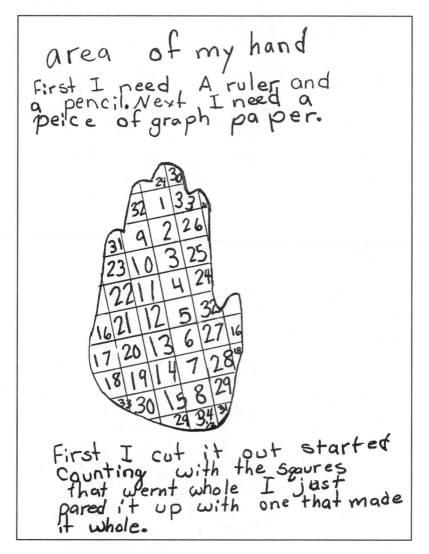

Lydia
GRADE 3, FEBRUARY

area of my hand

First I need A ruler and a pencil. Next I need a peice of graph paper.

First I cut it out started counting with the squares that wernt whole I just pared it up with one that made it whole.

Figure 24 This student gave the same numbers to pairs of partial squares, matching up parts that appeared to equal one whole.

Some children seemed to latch onto the graph paper idea only after they saw what their classmates were doing. They tended to count the whole or almost whole squares inscribed within their tracings and ignored the smaller partial squares. For these children, apparently, the square unit is an object that must remain intact to be meaningful (see Figure 25). If these children did not yet perceive a square as a unit of measurement, it was not surprising that they did not put together partial squares to create the equivalent of a unit.

570

575

Area of my hand

I am going to trach my hand to
solve my problom. I will use a peac of graff
paper.

51 Sqare's

Figure 25 Some children ignored partial squares and counted only whole or almost whole ones.

Soon it was time for the children to explain their strategies for finding the area of their hands and feet. When the children who used graph paper explained their thinking, there was a sudden burst of awareness and expressions of "Ah, now I get it!" and "Why didn't I think of that?" By the end of the discussion, all the children seemed to have a clearer understanding about finding the area of nonrectilinear shapes.

580

This investigation answered some of my initial questions. The children did use square objects to measure the area, even when they complained that their hands and feet were too "wavy." They seemed to understand that even the area of nonrectilinear shapes is measured using square units. But I'm left with questions about what they understand about partial squares. When a child writes, "With the squares that weren't whole, I just [paired] it up with one that made it whole," what does she understand about units of area that many of her classmates haven't yet thought about?

When we were figuring out the area of our square rug, the children could integrate the linear measurement of the sides with the area measurement. They created visual and mental arrays based upon the work we had done with arrays when we studied multiplication. Now, when confronted with shapes other than rectangles, they first tried to use linear measurements to determine area. It was as if they were asking themselves, "If the length of the sides is important in figuring out the area of the rug, why isn't it helping us figure out the area of our hands and feet?" I'll have the children address this question in their next math journal entry.

I have this nagging feeling that there are larger issues at work here, and I find myself still grappling with how to discover them. What kinds of activities can I conjure that will advance the thinking of those children who do not yet perceive the flexible nature of square units as measuring units? For now, these larger issues will remain on the tip of my mind!

585

590

595

600

605

5

From rectangles to triangles and trapezoids

In chapter 2, we saw how a variety of shapes can be decomposed into other shapes and then put back together. For example, in case 7, Andrea's students decomposed an oddly shaped region (the floor of their classroom) into familiar shapes, rectangles and triangles, in order to draw a map. In chapter 4, we saw how rectangles can be decomposed into arrays of squares, each square representing a unit of area. Structuring rectangles in this way brings us to the familiar formula, Area = length × width. That is, multiplying the linear dimensions of a rectangle yields the number of square units that constitute its area. In chapter 5, the concepts and skills developed in these earlier chapters are brought to bear to explore the areas of other shapes: triangles and trapezoids.

In Sally's case 22, the children consider a right triangle formed by dividing a geoboard in half.

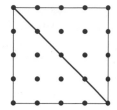

They realize there are different ways to determine the area of the triangle—to take half of the area of the square that is its double, or to count square units. However, unclear about how to work with partial units, the children come up with three different counts! They must reconcile their strategies to see that their different methods produce the same measure of area.

In Rachel's case 23, the children consider a variety of triangles, and in Sandra's case 24, trapezoids. These students also count square units and decompose regions as they move toward generalizing their methods for finding the area of triangles and trapezoids.

In each case, what do the children show us about the different ideas that must come together to find the area of a triangle or trapezoid? What generalizations do they make? And what new insights do you gain about the area of these shapes?

C A S E   22

Sometimes it's half and sometimes I'm confused

GRADE 4, MARCH

Yesterday my class worked with geoboards, finding and proving different ways to make halves. Today they continued the activity, using dot paper to model halves. Most of the proofs involved folding and covering. One student ventured to say that he thought he had another method of proof: If the smallest rubber-band square was one square unit on the board, then the whole board had sixteen square units and the half had eight.

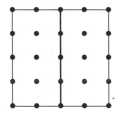

The next half we modeled on the overhead was a rotation of the first. The class saw that and made the same statements about the area.

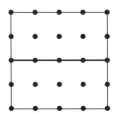

Our third model divided the geoboard into halves by cutting on the diagonal. The students knew it was half, because one could fold it to cover the other half.

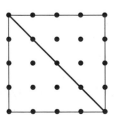

SETH: But what about the area idea?

MARIO: Yeah, it's not half.

SETH: When you fold it, it is half. Look.

Seth went to the overhead and demonstrated the congruence, but he said when you count the units, it's not half anymore. I asked if anyone else got Seth's idea, and there were students, more than I would have anticipated, who did! I asked one of them to explain.

KIRA: When you count the square units, there are only six, and you need eight to be half, so even though you can fold and prove it's half, sometimes it's not half.

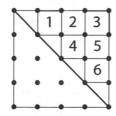

SHANNON: I disagree with Kira. When you count it, the area is ten, not six like Kira said, because you have to count all the pieces. But I do agree with her that sometimes this way of cutting it is half and sometimes it's not.

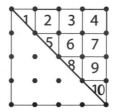

When Shannon finished speaking, I realized the P.E. specialist was standing at the door ready to take the class to gym. We had to end the conversation. Clearly, there was an idea here that these students needed to work through. As they were putting away their papers and pencils, Jay called out, "No, wait! I get it!"

We'll start with Jay's idea when we get back to this lesson tomorrow. I expect that he will help the class count half-square units, which will enable us to reconcile the difference between two methods of finding the area of the triangle: counting units, and decomposing the large square into two congruent triangles. Either way, the area is 8 square units.

Area of triangles

Rachel

GRADES 3 AND 4, MARCH

In our explorations with area and perimeter, we had done a lot of work with rectangles, including real-life math problems about carpeting a floor or tiling a room. Many of the kids were feeling that they understood area of rectangles. I decided it would be interesting to see how they thought about finding the area of a triangle. This case describes three lessons on that subject.

LESSON ONE

I drew a 3×4 rectangle on the board (with the grid showing) and asked what the area was.

I heard these answers:
  "12."
  "12 square tiles."
  "12 boxes."
  "3 by 4."

Clearly, we were ready to move on to triangles. I wanted to focus on how kids would think about finding the area of a triangle within the rectangle. Would they compare the two shapes? If you know the area of the rectangle, do you know the area of the triangle? We eventually got there, but it was quite a distance from where the class started.

I told the class we would be looking at triangles with the following restrictions: The triangle needed to fit inside the 3×4 rectangle; one side had to be the whole length of the rectangle; and the opposite vertex had to be in the middle of the opposite side of the rectangle. When drawn carefully, it looked like this:

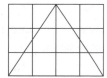

I asked the class to pair up to investigate the question, What is the area of the triangle? 60

They jumped up and got straight to work. Each pair had graph paper to draw on. As I listened on the periphery of conversations, I heard kids saying things like, "This is a quarter of a square," or "This is worth three quarters." They were making grand statements about each piece's worth, 65 and I found myself saying repeatedly, "Prove it."

When we came back to the meeting area, Tara was the first to share her proof. Having drawn her triangle within the larger rectangle freehand, the sides curved in a bit (see Figure 26), which led to an incorrect count.

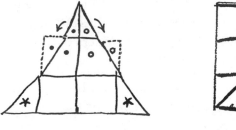

Tara's work   Thomasina's work

Figure 26 Tara and Thomasina both drew their rectangles and triangles freehand, leading to some inaccurate assumptions.

| TARA: | Two halves make a whole [starred triangles], and then we knew that these pieces [top two triangles] were quarters, and they fit here and here [completing the squares just below]. That makes 5. | 70 |

| TEACHER: | Are those pieces [top two triangles] really quarters? | |

| CLAIRE: | If it's not a quarter—if they fit, it doesn't matter if it's a fourth or not because it still makes a whole. | 75 |

Rachel

Thomasina had made the same error in her freehand drawing and offered an argument similar to Tara's. I was interested in how the kids were ascribing number values to pieces of squares within the triangle. Claire was more interested in the whole and not what each part was worth, but something in this idea seems very important. I'll have to pursue this topic in more depth at a later time.

Candace had originally been excited to share her proof, but her enthusiasm seemed to be waning, so I called on her to share before she gave up. She presented this picture.

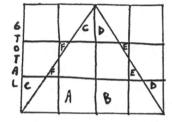

CANDACE: There are already two on the bottom [A and B]. And if you take these two [triangles C and D at the top] and put them on the bottom, that makes four. Then you take these [triangles E and F] and put them here [filling the top corners of the middle squares], which makes 6.

ZOE: First I thought definitely 5; now I'm not sure. So far no one has had this little corner yet [*referring to regions E and F in Candace's figure*]. We didn't use a ruler, did you?

Candace nodded. Indeed, Zoe, Thomasina, and Tara had all drawn in the triangles freehand. Candace had used a ruler to draw straight lines, so her drawing was more accurate.

At this point, a couple of kids spoke about how important it was to be exact. They all agreed that using a ruler would be important. Then Emil got back to the idea of how to find the area in the triangle.

EMIL: If you add the squares outside the triangle and add it to the triangle, you should get 12. So, since 5 + 7 = 12, you then want to get 7 on the outside.

Emil was still thinking that the area of the triangle would be 5, but Rashad picked up on the idea of looking outside the triangle and argued it should be 6.

Rachel
GRADES 3 AND 4, MARCH

RASHAD: The rectangle is worth 12. If you took the part that's not in
the triangle and folded it up [to put the two halves together],
it would make another equal triangle. The part in the middle
is 6, so each part is 6.

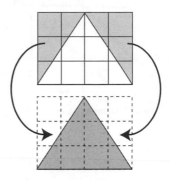

Rashad's remark came right at the end of the lesson. This day left me
with so much to think about: symmetry, whole/part relationships,
attributes of shapes, area, fractions, proofs, math materials, issues of
accuracy, and pedagogy. Had I given my students a carefully drawn
triangle on graph paper, would the same issues have come up? Or did the
fact that some children found 5 square units and others 6 put them into a
position where they couldn't simply rely on counting up squares and
matching parts? I'll see what comes up next.

LESSON TWO

One week later, we were ready to return to our investigation of the area of
a triangle. The whole class was gathered together in the meeting area
while I presented the task. Kids were working in pairs. Each pair had to
come up with any triangle inscribed within a 3 × 4 rectangle and find its
area. They were clear on the rules for making their own triangles: "any
triangle that uses one whole side and has a point on the opposite line."

The kids went off in their pairs. The attention and excitement was
palpable. Every kid had a starting place, and, with rulers or graph paper
in hand, they began the work.

We gathered again in the meeting area some time later. As each pair
presented results, I drew a representation of their work on the board. By
the end of the class, we were able to see each pair's drawing as part of the
whole visual representation of the class's work.

110

115

120

125

130

Ursula and Amy were the first to share. Their paper looked like this:

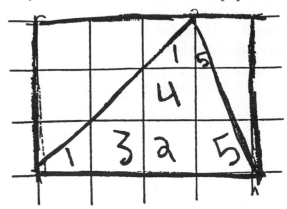

URSULA: I thought it was 6, but we don't have perfect proof. We tried to fit little teeny shapes into other shapes to make a full square. We tried to fit different mini-triangles into a square so it would be more simple.

TEACHER: How did you decide which mini-triangles to put together to make a square?

AMY: We didn't want to make a perfect triangle, we wanted to make it to the side. [*She is referring to the scalene triangle they drew, as opposed to the isosceles one I drew last week.*] So this one [top triangle 1] would fit down here [filling square 1 below], and this one [top triangle 5] down here [filling square 5 below].

Amy was pointing to the pieces within their triangle that would make a square when put together. I think when Ursula said they didn't have "perfect" proof, she meant that they'd only gotten to the "pointing" stage of their proof. That is, they could see by the accuracy of their drawing which pieces put together would make a square, but they hadn't actually proved it. They were convinced of the answer, but they hadn't collected evidence to prove it to anyone else.

Only as I'm writing this up do I see that Amy did not explain how she counted the sixth unit. This would have been particularly interesting since the two partial-units left do not fit together to make a square.

Claire and Jed were excited to share their work.

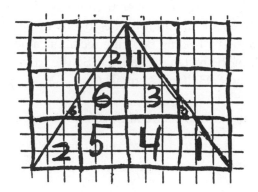

JED: We didn't think [the area] was 5 or 6 because there are really small triangles in the corners [the small pieces next to the squares labeled 6 and 3], and those really small ones don't fit into these [the upper left corner of square 6 and the upper right corner of square 3]. So we think it's like 5 and $\frac{99}{100}$ or something. It's too small to fit to make a whole, so it makes 5 and $\frac{99}{100}$.

Then Kathy and Brit showed their work:

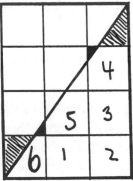

BRIT: We took this little black part here [above number 6] and it matches up here [to fill square 4]. And this shaded one [top right] matches up with this one [to fill square 6].

Brit didn't mention the third pair of triangles that would match up to fill square 5, but her argument seemed clear to the class. Then Claire picked up on Rashad's thinking of a week ago.

CLAIRE: Brit got the right answer, because all together there's 12 squares, and if you fold this together [that is, create the triangle by folding back the rectangle along its diagonal], it's half of the rectangle, so it's 6. So the triangle is half of this rectangle. Half of 12 equals 6.

170

Daphne brought us back to Claire and Jed's drawing.

175

DAPHNE: You can also fold an isosceles triangle in half, like in Claire and Jed's.

She made a gesture with her hand to show the imagined line of symmetry in their isosceles triangle.

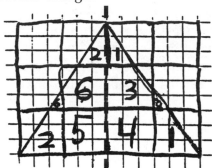

TEACHER: So, Claire, does that make you think any differently about the answer 5 and $\frac{99}{100}$?

180

RASHAD: It's just trying to figure out if the triangle space is equal to the space outside the triangle. So if you fold it, this space [inside the triangle] is the same as this part [the space outside of the triangle]. I think every single triangle in a 3×4 has to be 6, because I think you do it with all of them.

185

KRIS: I agree with Rashad totally, but you could make triangles that weren't 6 if you didn't use the whole side.

NOAH: I agree that all the triangles using the whole side and touching a point on the opposite side will always be 6 if they are drawn in super perfect. Because I'm pretty sure that you can't make a triangle that covers one side and touches another that is not 6.

190

Rachel

RASHAD: This is hard to see, but Kevin and I started with a rectangle and a triangle inside it, and then I cut it out. [*He shows the matching triangle he made with the "leftover" outside parts.*] These are the exact same triangles, so [the area] has to be 6 because they are both equal.

195

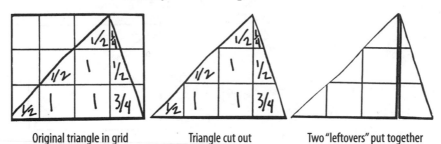

| Original triangle in grid | Triangle cut out | Two "leftovers" put together |

Rashad then put one triangle on top of the other to illustrate their congruence. (The fractional values he assigned to parts of squares in his diagram aren't quite right, but that didn't affect his demonstration.)

200

KEVIN: All the triangles are 6 because, if you cut the extra part that they left, they would all make half. So they are all 6.

LESSON THREE

By the end of that second lesson on the area of triangles, my students were all left with important ideas to ponder. Some were still thinking about how to match up pieces of squares in order to count the total. Others were making general arguments about why any triangle drawn according to our rules would have an area of 6 square units. A few students were ready to move on from there, so I met with them separately from the rest of the class.

205

210

I showed them two rectangles drawn on blank paper with the outside dimensions labeled.

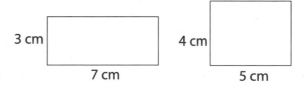

I then asked the kids to make their own triangles within the rectangles, using the now familiar rule: Use the whole side of a rectangle and any

215

point opposite that side. They had worked enough with this rule to feel comfortable launching straight into the project. They worked independently for a while and then shared their results.

Noah, who had made a right triangle by drawing a diagonal through the 4 cm × 5 cm rectangle, began by reading a general strategy he had written: 220

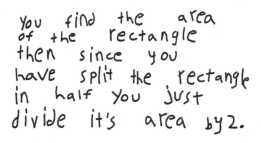 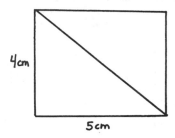

You find the area
of the rectangle
then since you
have split the rectangle
in half you just
divide it's area by 2.

Noah then looked over at Aaron's page and back at his own drawing, saying, "I think Aaron made different triangles, but he got the same answer." Aaron spoke up to explain his reasoning.

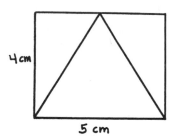

AARON: I just split it in half. 4 × 5 equals 20, and 20 divided by 2 equals 10. Both of these side things [the two triangles outside the isosceles] fit into this one [the isosceles], so it's half again. 225

TEACHER: How would you prove that the pieces outside the triangle are equal to "this one"?

Kris, looking at Aaron's work, offered a strategy. 230

KRIS: I would cut them out and fit them into each other.

Everyone agreed with Noah's generalization and Kris's strategy of cutting out and fitting triangles together. So, moving on, I pulled out a sheet with a triangle on it and asked the kids how they would figure out the triangle's area. There were only a few minutes of class left, but they were all interested in thinking about the question.

235

KRIS: [*measuring the base*] This is 5 centimeters.

RASHAD: Let's see how tall it is. [*He measures a line from the base to the opposite vertex.*] It's 3 centimeters.

KRIS: So it's 5×3. The answer is $7\frac{1}{2}$.

240

RASHAD: Umm, this triangle isn't exact.

NOAH: It only works if the triangle is equal. [*By "equal," he means isosceles.*]

KRIS: It should be equal if it's going to work. The little triangles both need to be $3\frac{1}{2}$.

245

Rashad had been working on his paper and the other children were looking on. He had drawn the full rectangle around the given triangle, and now he was calculating the areas of the external triangles.

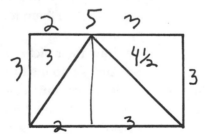

We were out of time, so the class ended there without an opportunity for me to ask the children what they meant. I think they had been expecting an isosceles triangle. If I had given them an isosceles with base 5 and height 3, then each of the external triangles would have been $3\frac{3}{4}$, slightly different from what Kris said. But I gave them a scalene triangle, and there was something left here for the children to sort out. They could follow through from Rashad's drawing. That will be our next lesson.

250

255

Area of trapezoids

Sandra

One part of the geometry and measurement curriculum is to develop the formulas for the area of various polygons. We started with the concept of area by counting squares on geoboard dot paper. The geoboard was new to many of the students, but they quickly learned to use the geoboard dots to form squares and then to find the area of polygons by counting full squares and equivalent squares (combining pieces to make squares). The students seemed to find the formulas for area of a triangle and area of a parallelogram fairly easily. In fact, many of them said they remembered doing much of this in previous grades but just needed a little reminding. | 260

Things got more interesting when we started to explore trapezoids. Students were assigned homework to create six different trapezoids on dot paper and find the area using the geoboard method. Then they were to try to find some rule or formula to make it possible to find area of a trapezoid without counting squares. I didn't expect everyone to find a rule, but I felt that the search would prepare them for the discussion in my next lesson. | 265 270

Sometimes I have the students draw their pictures or diagrams on the overhead transparencies, and sometimes I do the drawing. As I thought through what we would be doing in the coming lesson, I decided that I would do the drawing this time because I wanted the students to practice orally communicating the shapes and turns for the diagram. | 275

As class started, Molly was the first to offer a trapezoid for consideration. When I finished the drawing according to Molly's directions, it looked like this:

| MOLLY: | The area is 12 squares. Draw in the squares. See, there are ten full squares and four half squares, so the area is 12. But I don't see any base times height rule here. | 280 |

| TEACHER: | What is the base? | |

| MOLLY: | I think it's 8 because that's the bottom it's sitting on. The height is 2. | 285 |

I waited to see if she would go on before I pushed further.

| TEACHER: | Why? | |

| MOLLY: | If you pick a place on the base and go straight up, then you go up 2 to get to the top. | |

Most heads nodded in agreement, but this didn't seem very interesting. There was silence. Then... | | 290 |

| ASHRAF: | If you add the top and the bottom on Molly's you get 12, but that doesn't work for my trapezoids. | |

I then drew Ashraf's example, following his instructions.

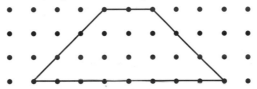

| TEACHER: | What's the area of this trapezoid? | 295 |

| ASHRAF: | It's 15 by counting squares, but I found another way that helped me. I split the trapezoid into a rectangle and triangles. I found the area of each piece, and then added them all together. | |

| TEACHER: | Will that method work on other trapezoids? | 300 |

I looked around the room at everyone as I asked the question and waited for a response. Many students were checking their diagrams to see if what Ashraf had said was true for theirs, too. I had half expected them to see this when they created their diagrams, but they seemed genuinely engaged in looking for the rectangles and triangles. Then Indra raised her hand. | 305

INDRA: Ashraf's way works for my diagrams, but I found another way. It's actually a rule that uses the numbers for the trapezoid to find the area. [*She pauses.*] First take the base and subtract the top. Take that answer and multiply it by the | 310 height, and then cut it in half. That answer is the area of the triangles all together. Then take the top times the height, and that is the area of the rectangle. Add the two answers together and you get the area.

TEACHER: How did you get that? | 315

INDRA: I just started trying different things with the numbers until I got the same answers as counting the squares. It worked for all six of my examples so... [*shrugs her shoulders*].

I had to think a moment, myself, about what Indra had said. I needed to see in my mind why the subtracting step would get the necessary | 320 number for finding area of the triangles. Aha! If you take out the rectangle that is in the middle of each trapezoid and then push the ends together, you have a triangle. Her method of top times height, plus base minus top times height divided by 2, would work!

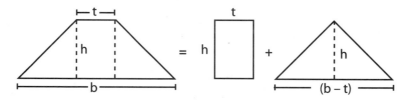

I asked two other students to repeat in their own words what Indra | 325 had just explained, and then had each pair of students in the class explain both Ashraf's and Indra's methods to each other.

TEACHER: Is there another way to find area of a trapezoid?

WALLACE: I think I have another way. I just checked both examples on the screen with my method, and mine gives the same area. | 330 Take the base and add the top. Take that answer and multiply by the height, and then take half.

Sandra

GRADE 7, JANUARY

TEACHER: Let's check the two trapezoids on the screen by using Wallace's method.

I walked around the room observing what types of trapezoids were on papers and how partners were checking Wallace's method. After it looked as though everyone had finished, I asked Wallace how he found his rule. 335

WALLACE: I started thinking about Ashraf's adding the top and bottom in Molly's trapezoid. Most of the formulas for area use times by height, so I did that, and then had to divide by 2 to get the right area. For Molly's problem, it didn't matter if you multiplied by the height because the height was 2. You just timesed by 2 and then divided by 2. That's just undoing the multiplying. 340

TEACHER: I noticed that all of the trapezoids that I saw on papers were the same kind. Mathematicians have a special name for those trapezoids. They call them isosceles trapezoids because the two nonparallel sides are congruent or equal in length. 345

I had decided during my walk around the room that I needed to expand the students' idea of trapezoid and that I would do it directly. I then drew several shapes on the transparency and identified them as trapezoids. 350

TEACHER: Your next assignment is to create three trapezoids that are *not* isosceles and find the area using the geoboard method. Then test both Indra's and Wallace's methods to see if they work on any kind of trapezoid. 355

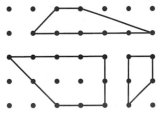

The next day, there was a mixed result. I saw a lot of trapezoids sitting on the longer of the two parallel sides, but they were not isosceles. The students seemed pretty smug and satisfied with themselves because the two methods worked for every trapezoid until… 360

KATE: I've got a trapezoid. Well, I think it's a trapezoid—but I can't figure out how to use either method.

I asked Kate to draw her figure on the transparency on the overhead and then everyone stared at it for a while.

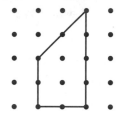

KATE: I know the area is 6, but I can't tell what the height is to try the two methods. 365

Class members were beginning to fidget uncomfortably. I had to make a decision quickly, not only to keep their attention but to decide how to wrap this up with just 10 minutes left in the class. They had made much progress in understanding area and finding formulas for areas of shapes, 370 including trapezoids.

TEACHER: When we had the two methods for area of trapezoids, we used the terms *base* and *top*. What can you tell me about the base and top of the trapezoids we looked at? [*Everyone responds with blank stares.*] Did you notice that the base and 375 top were the parallel sides?

A look of relief crossed Kate's face. I noticed that she and at least four other students were turning their heads sideways so as to make the parallel sides seem to be the top and bottom.

GREG: Do you mean that the base and top are always the parallel 380 sides? Is it like the baseball diamond is really a square, only tilted?

I nodded yes, and there was a noticeable lifting of tension in the room. Just in time!

Sandra

When I thought about my telling the students about the parallel sides, I wondered if I had stolen some of the joy of discovery from them. However, I decided that given limited time and the teachable moment, I did the right thing. The student journals that I read the following week reinforced my thinking. Seven of the 24 students wrote specifically about seeing the parallel sides in a new way so that the rules fit all trapezoids. Other students described the rules effectively, but pointed out that counting the squares was a much nicer way to find area. One student, Jake, wrote about the rules as being time-savers for him but posed a new problem:

I thought, Wow! The area is easy to find by counting squares. But exploring how to get the measure of the parallel sides and the height of this trapezoid will take a few more lessons! It will be a great lead-in for the Pythagorean theorem.

Measuring volume: Structuring boxes

How many cubic units constitute the volume of this box? If you can look at it only from the outside, how can you tell? What must we understand about the box in order reason this out?

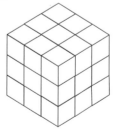

In chapter 4, we considered the challenge children face in learning to visualize a rectangular array—to recognize rows and columns and their coordination in a rectangle. Seeing this structure is key to keeping track of or calculating the number of squares used to cover a rectangular region, or in other words, finding the area of a rectangle.

With the introduction of the third dimension, children confront still further challenges to their ability to grasp spatial structure. In looking at a rectangular solid, they must see not only rows and columns, but also how those rows and columns form layers which, themselves, are stacked. These new feats of mental structuring must also include an awareness of parts of the shape that cannot be seen—the back faces, the internal space—but which must be imagined in relation to the parts that are seen.

In this chapter, children work on issues related to the question: How many objects are needed to fill a given box? In Terry's case 25, first graders see how many small boxes fit in a larger box. In Lydia's case 26, third graders estimate the number of acorns or tiles needed to fill a container. And in Lydia's case 27 and Rita Lucia's case 28, students take on the question posed above: If you can see only the surface of a box, how do you know the number of cubic units that fit inside?

As you read the cases, consider the following questions:

■ How do the children use layers, stacks, or slices to think about the volume of a container?

■ What are some ways of viewing a shape that lead children to incorrect conclusions about its volume?

Making, comparing, and packing boxes

GRADE 1, APRIL

My first graders, working in teams of two, were frantically trying to construct two different boxes out of twelve precut index cards (see Figure

27).* The classroom was humming with sounds of "This is hard," "You used my piece," and "We need more tape!" I was amazed at the level of enthusiasm and the way pairs of children were working strategically to figure out the puzzle of the rectangular pieces they found in their bags. What I saw in my classroom was almost identical to the descriptions I had read in the curriculum's accompanying Teacher Notes.

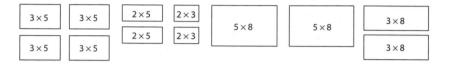

Figure 27 Each student pair had these twelve cards to make two different boxes. The dimensions, given here in inches, were not written on the students' cards.

I began to watch Rhea and John. John tends to jump in quickly and often works faster than his peers. Rhea is a more soft-spoken student who has learned how to work carefully in order to ensure her own understanding. Another characteristic I have observed over the year is that Rhea sticks closely to the guidelines given, whereas John tends to veer easily from the given directions and often invents his own twist on any given problem.

As I approached them, John had just returned to their work space and was showing Rhea how they needed to attach a handle to the top of the box they had assembled. He explained that it was too hard to tape on this last piece, so he wanted the box to be left open. Since Rhea wanted to use all the pieces, John thought a handle would be a good solution. She seemed to be following his explanation as he spoke to me.

The box they had successfully assembled was the larger of the two possible boxes, measuring $3 \times 5 \times 8$ inches. I suggested that they might want to work on the second box and leave their handle invention for another time. As I turned to observe other children, Rhea seemed ready to take on this task, but John continued to play with the handle he had made from a red pipe cleaner.

---

* "Making Boxes" from S. J. Russell, D. Clements, and J. Sarama, *Quilt Squares and Block Towns,* a grade 1 unit of *Investigations in Number, Data, and Space* (Glenview, IL: Scott Foresman, 1998).

Several minutes later I noticed that they had made both boxes, though one still had the "top" taped on only one edge. It lay on the table as though it were a chest with the top open. The smaller box, $2 \times 3 \times 5$, was nested inside the larger one. Rhea and John were beginning to play with their constructions when I sat down to ask them about their work. (For simplicity, the top flap on the larger box is not shown in the following diagrams.)

TEACHER: What do you notice about your boxes?

RHEA: One is bigger.

JOHN: They both have six faces.

RHEA: One of them, the top opens. The other is all taped up.

TEACHER: I noticed that you put one box inside the other one. How many boxes do you think will fit inside the bigger box?

Rhea picked up the smaller box that was nested inside, placed it back down in the center of the larger box and said, "One!"

John agreed, pulling the box closer to himself. "Yeah, one."

I was curious about their responses. Certainly the smaller box easily fit inside the larger one, but there was a lot of space left over. Might the children wonder about this extra space? I paused for a moment to think of a question that might encourage them to give more thought to the space inside the larger box. Finally I asked, "Do you think there might be more?"

JOHN: No.

RHEA: Wait, if you move this over, maybe we can fit another one in.

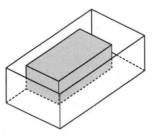
One smaller box fits inside.

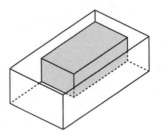
Rhea moves the box over.

She moved the smaller box so that one of its corners fit into a corner of the larger box.

As Rhea worked with the boxes, the larger one was resting with a 5×8 face flat on the table. The smaller box was resting on a 3×5 face. Upon pushing the smaller box into the corner, Rhea seemed to notice something else about the boxes. She said, "No, I can flip this up, and maybe there will be more." So saying, she changed the position of the smaller box. Now it was resting on a 2×5 face, still pushed into a corner of the larger box.

At this point John intervened with "No, we can move it around." He then rotated the smaller box so that it lay back on a 3×5 face, but was now lined up with the 5-inch length of the larger box.

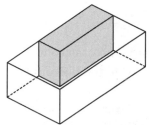

Rhea flips up the small box.

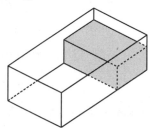

John rotates it and lays it flat.

But Rhea persisted, "We can still move it." She flipped the box again onto a 2×5 face and laid her hand along the top, suggesting by her motion that the tops of the boxes now met exactly.

RHEA: That's right. Now I think we can do two more.

TEACHER: Two more what?

RHEA: Two more boxes.

JOHN: We need more.

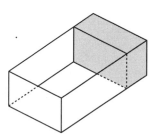

Rhea flips it up again.

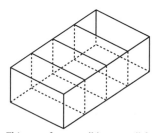

This way, four small boxes will fit.

With this, John raced to nearby tables where classmates had been assembling their boxes. He returned with two smaller boxes that other groups had made.

The class had not yet discussed the way the boxes were made; nor had we compared the boxes that each pair had assembled. Did John just intuitively know that all the "smaller" boxes were the same? Rhea never questioned him and gladly let him place the additional boxes in their "experiment" box. They soon had three identical $2 \times 3 \times 5$ boxes lying side by side, filling three-quarters of the larger box.

JOHN: Well, it's three.

RHEA: I think one more will fit.

JOHN: No, I don't think there's enough room.

RHEA: Yes.

JOHN: Oh, all right, I'll get one more.

Because of the way the children taped their boxes, some were more compact than others. I wondered if this mattered to John or if something else was getting in the way of his seeing that a fourth box would, indeed, fit. At the same time, I wondered, how did Rhea just seem to know this and accept it without needing to check?

When John got hold of a fourth box, it did just fit inside. I noticed he rotated it a little in his hand before he placed it carefully in the larger box to confirm Rhea's prediction. Even though exact dimensions were not written on the individual cards, I wondered if the children noticed that some of the faces were congruent. Is this what allowed for the interesting way Rhea and John flipped and rotated the smaller boxes to fit exactly inside the larger one?

I also wondered, if they had had a chance to compare the boxes in a whole group, whether anyone would have recognized that four of the smaller boxes were the same as one larger box. When this class has used geoblocks, they have often shown me they can find two or more blocks that, put together, "equal" a larger block. I have thought of this activity as composing and decomposing 3-D shapes. After watching Rhea and John manipulate their boxes, I see it now as an exercise in understanding volume. This experience stretched our box making much further than I had anticipated—and all because one of the boxes didn't have a top securely taped shut. It's amazing how and when learning takes place.

Acorns and tiles

Lydia

GRADE 3, SEPTEMBER

PART ONE: ESTIMATING ACORNS

It was the beginning of September, and I knew very little about my third   105
graders' mathematical thinking. I had a large bag of acorns for our science
unit on trees, so I began to think of ways to use the acorns in math. I was
intrigued by all the math that would be involved if I asked the children to
estimate how many acorns would fit inside a particular container.

I gave each team of two children a rectangular plastic container   110
holding a large handful of acorns. The containers varied in size; this way,
the emphasis would be on their strategy rather than on everyone's getting
the same answer. I was primarily interested in how the children would
estimate the number of acorns it would take to fill their container. None of
the containers held enough acorns to completely cover the bottom. I did   115
this intentionally because I wanted to see how the children would
visualize the acorns filling the container. I didn't want to push them into
thinking in terms of layers unless they discovered this for themselves.

I posed the following question: About how many acorns will fit inside
the container in front of you? Each team had a sheet on which they were   120
to use pictures, diagrams, and words to explain their thinking.

First I asked the children what I was asking them to do when I used
the word *about.* One of them told me it meant they were being asked to
estimate. In the ensuing discussion, the children gave several reasons why
it would be too hard to find an *exact* answer: 125

"The acorns are different sizes."

"The acorns are round, so there is space between them. You could
always push your finger in and make room for one more."

"You could put them over the top and they would still fit."

We decided to call each container "full" when the acorns were level   130
with the top edges.

Lydia
GRADE 3, SEPTEMBER

The teams were enthusiastic about starting. As I moved around the room, I noticed that most children first spilled their acorns onto the table to count them, then placed them back into the box. One team had placed the container of acorns behind them where they couldn't see it. When I asked why they had put the acorns out of sight, they said they thought they were supposed to *guess* how many would fill the container.

I quickly made a mental note that the class might need some help understanding the difference between guessing and estimating. I was reminded of the confusion that occurs when the routine meaning of a word collides with its mathematical counterpart. Has the word *guess* been used so often during estimating activities that its common usage overrides the specifics involved in its mathematical meaning? "Guess how many jelly beans are in the jar" is an example that comes to mind.

When a strategy is clearly unproductive, I always wonder what to do. When should I intervene, and when should I let the children discover for themselves the limitations of their approach? Although I was curious about what this team would do next, I felt it would be unfair to let them proceed when they had misunderstood the directions. So, I set them back on track.

After teams had counted their acorns and placed them back into their bin, differences in mathematical thinking really began to emerge. For example, Nick held up an acorn between his fingers.

NICK: It's about an inch long. [*He spreads his index finger and thumb apart about one inch, held vertically, then moves them along one side of the container.*] I think 10 is all that can fit on the bottom. I put my two fingers up the container and I got to 100.

Nick demonstrated, counting by 10. He had determined that the container was 10 acorns high. His written explanation is shown in Figure 28. Nick wrote as an estimate that 102 acorns could fit in his container. I was curious about where the other 2 acorns came from.

NICK: My partner said that maybe 15 acorns could fit on the bottom and I agree with him, so I put it between 100 and 105, so 102.

Although Nick knew that he would need to increase his final estimate to accommodate the additional acorns in his partner's estimate for one layer, he was unable to deal with the proportional differences in the

Lydia

Estimating Acorns

About how many acorns will fit in the container in front of you? _102_
Use the space below to explain your thinking. Use pictures and diagrams to help you explain your ideas.

I Estimating 102 becaues I tinke 10 on the botm. and I tinke 10 is all that could fit on the bottom, then I but my fingers up the container and I got to 100.

Figure 28 Nick estimates 102, and describes his estimating process of counting by tens (10 acorns in each of 10 layers).

estimates (changing from 10 acorns on the bottom to 15 would change the total from 100 to 150, not 105).

Edward was also using his fingers for measuring.

EDWARD: I counted all the acorns on the bottom now and thought, How many would fit on the whole bottom? It looks like 15 would fit. I used my finger and put it on top of one of the acorns to figure out how many layers there are. [*Edward's procedure is similar to Nick's.*] My finger would go up 5 layers of acorns, so my estimate would be 5 times 15—15, 20, 25, 30, 35. [*He pauses.*] No, that's by 5.

I checked with Edward later and saw that he next correctly counted by 15 and recorded his estimate of 75 on his paper (see Figure 29).

I was intrigued by what the next two teams were doing. Both teams turned their containers on one side to see how many acorns would fit when pressed in one layer against this side face. On one team, Anabel and Tiara then took a ruler and measured the length of the container. Anabel told me, "We had 15 acorns, and we put them all on one side. We could see that more than 15 acorns could fit on that side. The container is 8 inches long, so we figured 8 times somewhere around 15.

Tiara explained, "We pretended to move the acorns with our fingers. We got eight walls."

170

175

180

185

144   Measuring Space in One, Two, and Three Dimensions

Lydia

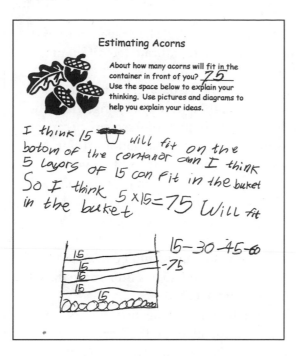

Figure 29 Edward also estimated a bottom layer, then figured the total amount for five layers high.

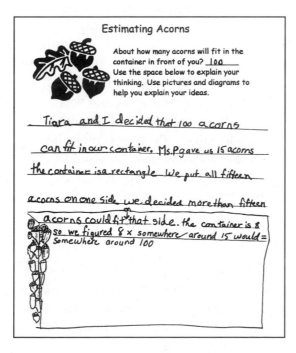

Figure 30 Anabel and Tiara's work shows one of their vertical layers, or "walls."

Lydia

GRADE 3, SEPTEMBER

When I asked Tiara what she meant by "walls," she moved her hand across the inside of the container eight times to indicate the different vertical layers she was imagining.

Anabel and Tiara were the only ones who visualized vertical layers in their container. When I first visited them, they were grappling with how many acorns they would need to cover the bottom of their bin, because the acorns they had covered less than a quarter of the bottom. Their container was a long, shallow, rectangular prism that had two vertical faces much smaller than the base. I can't help but wonder if they used the side of the bin to visualize vertical layers in direct response to their inability to estimate the number of acorns in the bottom, given so few acorns.

I asked them how they decided their estimate would be near 100. Anabel explained, "Well, 10 times 10 is 100, and 15 is a little more than 10, and 8 is a little less than 10. So it's around 100."

Ilsa and Sydney were also pressing their acorns against the sides of their container, a cube. They tipped the container on the first of four faces, placed enough acorns inside to completely cover the face, counted the number of acorns, and then tipped it on another face and repeated the process, doing this four times. Ilsa said, "If you gave us 82 it would fit the whole cube—22 four times is 82."

This team needed to place the acorns on each side to confirm that the sides were all the same size. Unlike most of the other teams, Ilsa and Sydney did not deal with the space in the middle of their cube. They counted only the acorns that fit against the four vertical faces. I was curious about what they would do later when asked to find the number of cubes in a 3-D array. Did the lack of uniformity of the acorns make it harder for them to visualize the middle of the container? Or would they have done the same thing with the congruent cubes? They realized their mistake the next day when they actually filled their container with acorns to test the accuracy of their estimating strategy. As Sydney said, "It didn't work because there was a hole where the acorns didn't fill. We only filled the sides and not the middle."

Most teams figured out how many acorns would fit on the bottom layer by seeing whether the acorns covered almost half or less than half of the bottom. Half seems to be a landmark quantity for many of them. They mentally added more acorns to fill the bottom, then either multiplied, used skip counting, or did repeated addition to see how many acorns would fill the container, layer by layer.

Ben used a different approach to estimate the number of acorns it would take to cover the base of his container. He pushed his 16 acorns to one side of the rectangular bin and figured that they covered one-third of the bottom. In his diagram (see Figure 31), he marked his container in thirds across the bottom, then added two layers above the bottom layer. He labeled each third in each layer with the number 16. He then added a column of nine 16s to get his estimate of 144 acorns. When we tested our estimates the next day, his was off by only *two* acorns.

230

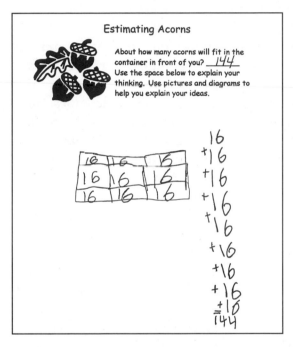

Figure 31 Ben's 16 acorns filled one-third of the bottom, and he worked from there.

This activity provided a great deal of information about the mathematical thinking of my third graders. All were able to skip count by 5 and 10. Most used landmark quantities either to help them estimate or to figure out their total number of acorns. What surprised me the most was that the majority were able to visualize and mentally reconstruct the whole and its parts in a very organized way. Most used the word *times* to indicate the multiplication involved when dealing with the "layers," "levels," or (my favorite) "walls" they were imagining. Most teams could find their estimates by using either repeated addition or mental math strategies. Some represented the calculation as multiplication.

235

240

Lydia
Grade 3, September

But what about those children whose approach to the acorn problem was either haphazard, inefficient, or unproductive? Derek and Erin were two such children. Shortly after the activity began, they abandoned their task and separately found more interesting things to pursue, unrelated to math. About a week later, we investigated volume again, this time with pennies instead of acorns. And again, Derek and Erin appeared first frustrated, then disinterested. When asked to estimate how many pennies were in a jar, Erin voiced her frustration, saying, "I bet there are 200 because the jar is very small. I just think that there are 200 in there, and that's all I'm going to do."

Meanwhile, Derek had taken the jar, dumped out the pennies, and was counting them one at a time. He was going to be sure to get it right this time!

I thought about the similarities in these two estimating activities. On both occasions, we had estimated with round objects as units. Did the fact that they were round make it difficult for Erin and Derek to visualize them filling their containers? Does the space that exists between round objects in a container make it difficult for some children to apply a layering approach to estimate volume? Was it impossible for children like Derek and Erin to mentally line up the acorns in arrays because of their shape?

I decided to set up an activity that I hoped would answer some of these questions. I wondered what would happen when I asked Erin and Derek to estimate a volume using one-inch-square color tiles that would fit together neatly, eliminating the space left between round objects. Would the square tiles enable them to mentally construct rows or layers in a way that the acorns had not?

PART TWO: ESTIMATION REVISITED

About a week later, while my student intern was reading a story to the class, I asked Erin and Derek to come with me to a small room off the library where we would do some math together. They were enthusiastic about accompanying me.

I gave each child a clear rectangular container and a handful of color tiles. As with the acorns, there were not enough color tiles to cover the bottom of the container, but both children had enough tiles to place along at least one edge of their container, should they decide to do so.

Measuring Space in One, Two, and Three Dimensions

The color tiles did not fit perfectly along one edge in Erin's container, so she had to deal with either leftover space or overlapping tiles. I was interested in investigating these questions:

■ Even though the tiles fit edge to edge, how will Erin deal with the leftover space or overlapping tiles at the corners of her container?

■ Given square objects, would the children estimate the volume in a more mathematical way than they had with the acorns and pennies?

■ How would the children estimate the number of color tiles that could fit on the bottom of the container?

■ Would they then use their estimate of the area of the bottom in order to estimate the number of tiles it would take to fill the container?

Erin dumped the color tiles out of her container. She placed four back inside, along the bottom edge, with the last two overlapping.

ERIN: I put some in to know how many went down a side. I put 4 down this side and [*she notices the small overlap*] even though it's not even, it's close enough. I counted 4 four times and got 16.

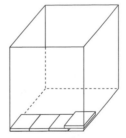

I then asked Erin if she knew that about 16 would fit on the bottom, how many would it take to fill the whole container?

ERIN: I'm not doing that; it's too hard! [*She pauses.*] I can do that. I'll pile... I don't have enough tiles. Can I grab some to help me?

She took a few more handfuls and piled tiles on top of each other in her container, forming one tall column that reached to the top.

ERIN: It's 27 layers high. What is 27 times 16?

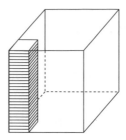

Erin started to write the numbers down in her math journal. I asked if she would like to use a calculator, but she said that she wanted to figure the answer out herself. As Erin started to write, I turned to Derek. | 305

Derek had also dumped the tiles out of his container (he had five) and placed four on the bottom of his container. First he arranged the four tiles in a 2×2 array. | 310

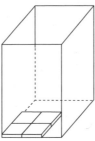

DEREK: [*to himself*] This won't help me.

TEACHER: Why?

DEREK: It didn't make sense to me, so I took one off the middle and moved it here.

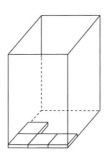

Derek took the middle tile in the second row and moved it to form one | 315
row against one edge. I was encouraged that Derek was aware of the need
to figure out how many tiles fit along an edge. He then took the

remaining tile from the table and placed it in the second row. He started to move the tiles around again, but my watching him seemed to make him nervous, so I returned to Erin.

What I saw Erin do next made me completely rethink my assumptions about the limitations of her mathematical thinking. She had three multiplication problems written down in her math journal, and she explained them to me.

$$\begin{array}{r} 27 \\ \times\, 10 \\ \hline 270 \end{array} \qquad \begin{array}{r} 27 \\ \times\, 5 \\ \hline 135 \end{array} \qquad \begin{array}{r} 27 \\ \times\, 1 \\ \hline 27 \end{array}$$

ERIN: I couldn't do 27 × 16, so I knew that when I count by ten 27 times I get 270. [*She shows me how she counts by ten on each finger.*] 10 tens is 100, so 20 tens is 200, and 7 more tens is 270. Then I counted by 5 on my fingers: 10 fives is 50, so 20 fives is 100, and 7 more is 135. Then I have to add another 27.

Erin then added 27 and 135 and got the correct sum of 162. To add 162 and 270, she further decomposed her partial products, adding the 100 (from the 162) and the 200 (from the 270) to get 300, then added the remaining 70 and 62 with the correct answer of 432.

While I checked in with Derek, Erin decided to figure out how many color tiles would fit in four containers. I had to remind myself that this is the same child who seemed to shut down during our first two estimation activities.

Derek was not able to figure out how many color tiles would fit on the bottom of the container by moving around the five he had. The breakthrough that I thought was about to occur had not! Derek has a diagnosed learning disability in the area of visual and spatial perception, so I was very impressed by what I saw next. To compensate for his difficulty in seeing how the tiles fit together in the container, he traced the bottom of the container on a page in his math journal. Next he traced the color tiles inside the tracing of the container and saw that three fit neatly in one row. From what he said next, this may be the first time he realized that there was any order to the tile arrangement:

DEREK: I was going to erase one square [*he has drawn three rows of three*], but 3 and 3 is 6, so it has to be 9.

Lydia

GRADE 3, SEPTEMBER

TEACHER: What helped you see it has to be 9?

DEREK: The squares are in a line, so if I have 6, there's 3 more over here [*pointing to last row*].

Derek seemed very pleased with himself. I was aware of the mental fatigue he might have been feeling, but I decided to ask him how he might figure out how many tiles would fit in the whole container. He had seen Erin stack the tiles up in her container and decided to do the same thing. In one corner of his container he carefully stacked 29 tiles to the top and stopped. I asked him again how many tiles it would take to fill the container. In his math journal, he had a page of his double facts from 1 to 50. He found the 29 + 29 = 58 and then took out a calculator. He added 58 + 58 = 116, 116 + 116 = 232, 232 + 232 = 464. I asked him how he would know when to stop, and he replied, "I can't get it into my head any more."

We decided to stop, but before returning to the classroom, I decided to ask the children about estimating acorns. Both agreed that the acorn activity was harder. I asked why.

ERIN: The acorns aren't the same size and shape. They're not flat. It wouldn't fit the same. They're not square.

DEREK: It was really complicated for me. The acorns are really small. Cubes [*meaning tiles*] are flat and big and long.

Although Erin and Derek demonstrated very different levels of conceptual understanding, this activity seemed to advance the mathematical thinking of each child in a way that the acorn and penny activities had not. When given the square tiles, Erin was immediately able to visualize a 4×4 array on the bottom layer and use that information to visualize 16 stacks of 27 tiles. Although it was not yet clear whether Derek could visualize either the vertical stacks or horizontal layers of tiles that would fill his container, he had a major breakthrough in his understanding of rectangular arrays. He recognized the ordered rows of tiles that he had traced and could represent this arrangement numerically as $3 + 3 + 3 = 9$.

I am reminded of the importance of providing students with the support or "scaffolding" they might need if they are to find an entry point into a mathematical investigation. It is clear that some children in my

classroom need more experiences estimating objects that can be arranged | 385
neatly within a space. By concretely manipulating rectangular objects
within a given space, they are better able to recognize the order of their
arrangement, as Derek demonstrated. They are then (as Erin demonstrated) able to use that arrangement to mentally visualize what the rest of
the space in the container will look like when filled. This activity enabled | 390
both children to move closer to a more complete understanding of
volume.

CASE 27

The color-cube sandwich

Lydia

GRADE 3, MAY

This year I have become very interested in observing and interviewing my
students to determine why some of them have difficulty visualizing the
space inside common three-dimensional shapes, such as cubes and rectan- | 395
gular prisms. I have been particularly interested in the thinking of one of
my students, Derek.

Derek has demonstrated repeatedly this year the need to have multiple
concrete experiences with objects before he can interpret symbolic repre-
sentations. For example, only after numerous attempts at building two- | 400
dimensional arrays with color tiles and then tracing these arrangements
on paper was Derek able to see the order in the arrangements. Derek can
now create concrete arrays for multiplication facts such as 3×4, but this is
still a new concept for him. When asked to describe how many blocks are
in his array, Derek will often revert to counting them one at a time, | 405
whereas most of his peers would say, "That's 3×4, so the answer is 12."

I have watched with interest the slow but steady development in
Derek's thinking as we extended our investigation from two-dimensional
to three-dimensional shapes. During each investigation of volume in my
class this year, Derek has been unable, and often unwilling, to predict the | 410

number of cubes that would fill a container. Instead, he has insisted on filling the container, dumping out the contents, and then counting the cubes one by one.

Derek's growing understanding of two-dimensional arrays has informed his thinking about volume in interesting ways. In one investigation last month, students were to predict how many one-inch color cubes could fit in a small cardboard box. Immediately, Derek tried to scoop up all the color cubes he could find in order to fill the box. This time when I stopped him, he lined up cubes along two adjacent edges inside the box. For the first time, he could visualize the 11 × 7 rectangle they would create when filled in.

DEREK: There's 11 here [*pointing to the cubes along the long edge*], so there's 11 here and here and here… [*pointing to an imaginary line of cubes extending from each of the 7 cubes along the width*].

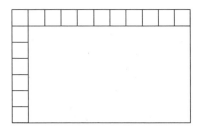

Using color cubes, Derek then created the entire 11 × 7 rectangle in the box. The box could hold another layer of 77 cubes, but when I asked Derek about how many more blocks he would need to fill the box, he acted frustrated and just continued to collect cubes to fill the box. It seemed that Derek was not yet able to visualize the box as composed of rectangular layers.

One day shortly before Derek's work with the cubes in the cardboard box, I noticed him alone at a table in the back of the room. Just as I was about to remind him to get back on task, I observed that he was filling a 10 × 5 × 3-inch clear plastic container with color cubes, arranged neatly in stacks of different colors. As I worked with another group, I periodically looked up and watched as Derek turned the container and peered through the clear plastic at each of the faces.

Lydia

GRADE 3, MAY

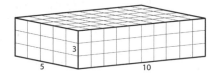

The filled container has been sitting in the front of the room for a few weeks now. On one recent inspection of his container, Derek noticed some missing cubes. "Someone took three yellow cubes out of my box!" he announced.

It had been a while since we had done any work with volume. Yesterday, I decided to spend a few minutes with Derek and his container of color cubes. After engaging him in small talk for a few minutes, I asked him why he decided to fill the container with cubes.

DEREK: I just feel like building.

Interested in how he would describe his arrangement of cubes, I asked him how the cubes were arranged in his container.

DEREK: There's ten that go in a straight line [*pointing down the length*]. There's only five that go across [*tracing his finger along the width*]. In the sides, there's only three. [*He stacks three cubes vertically outside the container*].

I could barely contain my excitement that Derek had, for the very first time, identified volume by the three dimensions that define it! I wondered if he would see the relationship between these dimensions and the volume if I asked him to tell me how he could figure out how many cubes are in the container. Remembering how he originally figured this out, he told me, "I counted how many go straight across because I wanted to figure out how many were in here. So I took out all the blocks, counted them, and got 150."

One of the most difficult aspects of teaching for me is knowing what questions to ask. This was one of those times. I wanted to probe Derek's thinking without asking him a question that might force him to abandon his natural way of thinking.

Finally I asked if there was any way Derek could show me how he counted 150 blocks without taking them out of the container.

DEREK: You could count by the lines going straight. You could count
              by this 10 row [*pointing to the rows in the top layer*]: 10, 20, 30,
              40, 50.

He then turned the container so that a long side was facing him, and
continued counting 60, 70, 80.

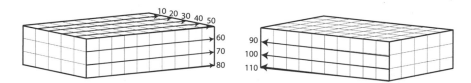

Turning the container so that the other long side was facing him, he
counted 90, 100, 110.

Next Derek turned the container so that the short side was facing him.
He pointed through the plastic and added on the five vertical stacks of
three cubes: 113, 116, 119, 122, 125.

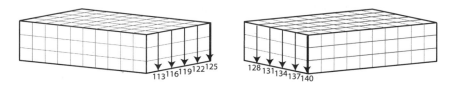

And finally, turning the container so that the other short side was
facing him, he counted five more stacks of three: 128, 131, 134, 137, 140.

Derek looked at me quizzically, because he knew there were 150 blocks
in the container, not 140. "Wait. Did I do this side?"

To determine the volume of the container, Derek counted only the faces
of the blocks he could see on the top and along the four sides of the
container. This is a common mistake that many of my students made early
in the year during our first investigations of volume. In September, some
of my third graders also ignored the middle of the solid and based their
count on the number of cubes along the faces. Like Derek, they, too,
ignored the bottom face. Since then, they have developed a solid understanding of volume, so I was optimistic that this error signified that
Derek's thinking was moving in the right direction.

I asked him what he hoped he would get as his answer, and he
confirmed that he was expecting to get 150. He was clearly disappointed
and increasingly frustrated. Creating the arrays in this container had

meant a lot to Derek, and I felt compelled to end his experience on a happy note. So, I asked him what his favorite sandwich was. (Stay with me here.) "Fluff," he told me.

We talked about how you make a fluff sandwich with bread on the bottom, then a layer of fluff, and then another piece of bread on the top. I asked him to think about the cubes in his container as a fluff sandwich. I held out my hand, palm up, and asked him to show me where the bread would be on the model.

DEREK: The bottom is bread. It's 50. The top is 50, too. That's 100.

TEACHER: Do we have 100 cubes in our sandwich?

DEREK: Yes—wait, no. We need the fluff! 100 plus 50 [*pointing to the middle layer of cubes that shows along the outside of the clear container*] is 150.

Derek smiled, and I couldn't help wondering what he'll do the next time he's confronted with a volume problem. What kind of sandwich will he make then?

CASE **28**

How many cubes fill the box?

Rita Lucia

GRADE 5, FEBRUARY

I was working with my fifth graders on a unit in which students develop strategies for determining the number of cubes needed to fill paper boxes.* This was our first experience with volume this school year, so I

---

* "How Many Cubes?" from M. Battista and M. Berle-Carman, *Containers and Cubes,* a grade 5 unit of *Investigations in Number, Data, and Space* (Glenview, IL: Scott Foresman, 1998).

was unsure how these activities would progress. The first activity was to look at a pattern that could be folded up to create an open box.

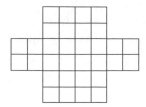

The children were to predict how many cubes were needed to fill the box, then copy the pattern onto graph paper, cut it out, tape it together to form a box, and fill it with cubes. In this way students verified their predictions. | 515

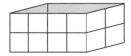

In a follow-up activity, students created their own patterns on graph paper, estimated the number of cubes that would fit, constructed the boxes, and then filled them with cubes to test their predictions again. | 520
Throughout these activities, the children knew they were working to develop a strategy for predicting how many cubes were necessary to fill a box. Their strategy had to work for *any* box, not just one particular box.

After several days of these activities, I decided to have a conversation with three boys in the group. Two of them had developed methods to | 525
predict the number of cubes required to fill a box, and they seemed confident and ready to defend their methods, but the third boy had encountered difficulties in the predicting and constructing activities. I wanted to understand what they knew, how they knew it, and what some children understood that made them more successful at finding a strategy. | 530
That is, what do Efren and Orlando look at and understand that Leo doesn't? What is Leo thinking about, or not thinking about, that makes these tasks so troublesome for him?

I displayed a box made from a pattern and asked them to show on paper—with pictures, words, and numbers—their strategy for deter- | 535
mining the number of cubes needed to fill the box. I also asked the boys to relate orally what they had written on their papers. Efren wanted to share first. He was eager, so I assumed he knew his plan worked.

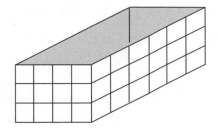

EFREN: I counted the bottom and there were 24 squares. That is kind of a layer on the bottom. Then I saw that the sides were all three high. So then I thought, I need two more layers of 24 cubes to fill up the box. It is 72.

540

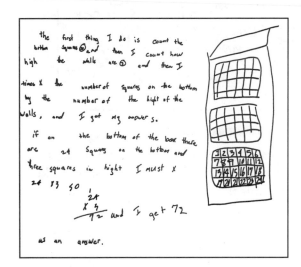

Figure 32 Efren saw the $6 \times 4 \times 3$ box as three layers of 24.

Efren's written explanation in Figure 32 reads as follows:

The first thing I do is count the bottom squares (24) and then I count how high the walls are (3) and then I times × the number of squares on the bottom by the number of the [height] of the walls and I get my answers. If on the bottom of the box there are 24 squares on the bottom and three squares in [height] I must × 24 × 3 so

545

$$\begin{array}{r} 24 \\ \times\,3 \\ \hline 72 \end{array}$$ and I get 72 as an answer.

550

Orlando then described his strategy to us (see Figure 33).

ORLANDO: I looked at the bottom of the box, too, and I counted—1, 2, 3, 4, 5, 6—and when I got to the end, I kept on counting up the side—1, 2, 3. So I said, 3 times 6 is 18. Then I looked at the bottom again and counted four across, so I knew that I need 4 groups of 18. The answer is 72.

555

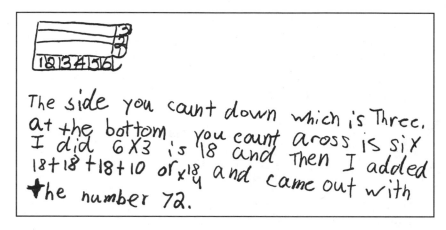

The side you caunt down which is Three. at the bottom, you count aross is six I did 6 X 3 is 18 and Then I added 18+18+18+10 or x18/4 and came out with +he number 72.

Figure 33 Orlando saw the 6 × 4 × 3 box as four vertical layers of 18.

I think both boys' strategies are very similar; they saw the cubes in layers inside the box. Efren's layers are horizontal "flat layers," or "like slabs one on top of the other," he calls them. Orlando's are vertical.

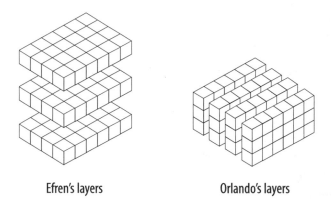

Efren's layers   Orlando's layers

Now it was Leo's turn. Leo told us that you count the bottom and all the squares on both ends and the long sides and add them up. That, he said, tells you how many cubes you need to fill the box. He believed you need 54 cubes. I noticed that while he wrote "I counted the *ends* [and] the *sides*," using the plural (see Figure 34), he clearly counted only one side (12) and one end (18). Although his plan was incorrect, he didn't even follow it in this instance.

Figure 34 Leo counted the squares on three faces.

Overall, I wondered how Leo was looking at this box. I don't think he realized that this three-dimensional box was more than just two-dimensional rectangles taped together. He didn't seem to have the conceptual understanding that when a two-dimensional pattern is cut out and taped together to form a three-dimensional shape, some new entity is created; it has a new attribute. The box now has volume. I thought Leo had a view that one cube was sitting on each square of the pattern. When the pattern was cut and taped together into a box, he figured those cubes were now on the inside of the box, filling it completely. He didn't see that there would be some space inside of the box that had not existed beforehand.

I had to help Leo think about the inside of the box. I decided to show him what would happen if you try to fill the empty box with the number of cubes he predicted in the exact way he had counted them. Would this help him visualize?

I took the 24 cubes he said were on the bottom and put them on the bottom of the box. I took the 12 cubes for the end and lined them up against one end of the box. Of course, I needed to add only 8 cubes, and Leo noticed this. I took 18 cubes for the side, but needed only 10 to cover what was left of the side. He saw that also. Now I pointed out that the box was not full; there was still space inside the box. This really helped Leo to see his plan would not work, but he didn't say anything. I had the sense he was pondering what he had just seen.

The next day I gave Leo a $3 \times 3 \times 2$ box. After our session yesterday, he needed the chance to try again. Overnight, he had time to contemplate a new approach, and I hoped a smaller box might facilitate his visualization. I gave him the box with the cubes already in it and asked him to tell me how many cubes were needed to fill the box. He dumped them out and started counting,1, 2, 3..., but before he finished, he looked at the box and said, "Oh, I can count them by twos because the box is only two high." He connected the cubes in pairs and started to count by twos.

Before Leo finished counting, I stopped him and took the cubes away. I said, "Look at the box, Leo. See if you can tell how many cubes you think will fill the box."

I was elated to see Leo take the box in his hand and count: "2, 4, 6, 8, 10, 12, 14, 16, 18—18 cubes."

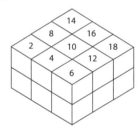

This showed some progress in Leo's thinking about three-dimensional shapes and volume. He used a strategy that showed he was thinking of the box as more than five two-dimensional rectangles. Before, he had been seeing the sides as two-dimensional arrays of cubes and not "seeing" the inside of the box at all. His counting by groups of two showed a new recognition—that there were cubes in the middle of the box, too.

Although Leo was progressing slowly in his understanding of volume, I was not worried that his pace was slower than I might hope. I didn't want him to adopt a strategy for finding volume that he hadn't thought about himself. I felt I needed to check my own inclination to show him some efficient method to accomplish this. Instead, I needed to provide some experiences to help him work his own way to understanding. With this most recent work, his view of the box changed from the first day of our activities, yet his view still differed from Efren's and Orlando's. What made him gain new perspectives? Was it my giving him the activity with the smaller box, or hearing his classmates' discussion of their ideas?

C H A P T E R

7

Same shape, different measures

In chapter 1, children explored different aspects of size. For example, Barbara's kindergartners saw that their foot could be measured by the number of cubes necessary to span its length, by the number of pompoms required to fill the space it occupies, or by the number of objects needed to ring it—length, area, and perimeter. Beverly's kindergartners saw that two boxes could be compared by length or by the number of cubes they held (volume).

Furthermore, we saw that ordering by size depends on which aspect of the objects are compared. Olivia's students discovered that the order of a set of rectangles changed, depending on whether they compared heights or areas. Beverly's students saw that, of their two boxes, the one with the longest dimension did not hold the most cubes.

In this chapter, we bring these measures together again to explore their complex and sometimes surprising relationships. In Tamara's case 29, students notice that figures with different areas can have the same perimeter. In Suzanne's case 30, they are surprised to see that rectangles with the same area can have different perimeters. In Bobbie's case 31 and Lucy's case 32, students consider the surface area of different cube structures.

As you read these cases, keep track of the different observations students make as they work with perimeter and area or surface area and volume. Which make you curious to investigate further?

The corner of area

Tamara

GRADE 5, NOVEMBER

I wandered into the classroom next to mine to admire some students' work: beautifully executed drafts of playgrounds on graph paper. As a former art teacher, I was immediately taken by the precision, thoughtfulness, and beauty of the exhibit. As a current math teacher, I wondered what the math plan was for this amazing project. When my colleague, Ms. Flores, saw how intrigued I was by the project, she invited me into her mathematics class.

The children had been working on their individual parts of the playground, but on the day I showed up, Ms. Flores had pulled the group together to look at one specific piece of the playground because she noticed some confusion about how to measure its perimeter. Ms. Flores stood at the board and drew a picture that represented the top view of an L-shaped wall. She asked the class, "How do you find the perimeter of this figure?"

Madeline went to the board and began drawing short lines to mark off units as she counted them.

5

10

15

When she rounded the corner, she said, "You still count this one [*pointing to the second side of the corner square*], but not this line [*she makes an X on the inner side of that square*] because it's not facing out." Madeline was aware of, and pointed out, the potential confusion that one square counts as two units of perimeter. I wondered whether this issue, or conflict, made moving from perimeter to area and back a tricky thing for some kids.

Ms. Flores then asked whether there was another way of coming up with the perimeter. I was interested in the question, but I didn't get why she asked it. Madeline had already explained that the perimeter was the outside lines, not the inside lines, making the perimeter 16 units. What more was there to say? I was surprised to see Phineas's hand go up. He came to the board and shared his thinking.

PHINEAS: I think of it as 4 × 4. There are these four lines here [outside of one leg], these four lines here [outside of the other leg], and these make up four [inside and end of one leg] and so do these [inside and end of the other leg]. And can I show you something else? This square [*he draws a 4 × 4 square*] has the same perimeter but a different area from the original shape.

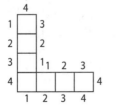

The other kids seemed mesmerized by what Phineas had just said. Then Eli waved his hand and called out, "I get it. Look at this." He made his forefinger and thumb into an L and flipped them to indicate the sides of a square. Ms. Flores looked confused. Eli leapt up to the board to show her his idea. On his way up there, Ivy handed him two craft sticks.

ELI: Look, you just pull this out. It's still the same perimeter, but not the same area. You see? You just pull these same lines out.

Eli put the craft sticks along the inside edges of the original figure, 3 units long, and then he flipped them up to make the square. The sticks fit perfectly into the space, and I kept wondering where those sticks had materialized from. The whole thing looked choreographed.

PHINEAS: Exactly. Now look at this, will you?

Phineas drew a picture, labeling the inner edges of the L-shape with the letters A and B. He showed that when the sticks were "flipped," they created a 3 × 3 square that fit into the L.

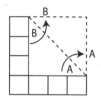

PHINEAS: You can just get rid of the square.

MS. FLORES: How can that be?

PHINEAS: It's a weird math world out there. [*Everyone laughs.*]

So as I think about this work I've observed, almost as a voyeur, I am struck by how one large, impressive playground project got whittled down to looking at two squares: the little one in the corner of the L, and the 3 × 3 that didn't actually exist except as a construction for understanding the original shape and its perimeter.

In my own class of third and fourth graders, we will be doing a quilt project with squares. I am interested to see if any of these issues come up for my students. Will they have to struggle with what the perimeter is? with what the area is? Will they have issues with the corner squares and measurement? I can't wait to find out.

How much skating space?

Suzanne

During the week before February vacation, I began a project that I hoped would help my students devise strategies for comparing the areas of irregular shapes, like skating ponds. I gave them construction cutouts of irregular shapes to represent ponds, and I presented a story about Carlos and Vanessa, who wanted to choose the largest pond for a skating rink.

Over several days, the children worked with partners on this problem. I saw them trying to measure, or at least cover, the internal space of the ponds with manipulatives that were uniform in size (connecting cubes, square-inch tiles, buttons). Many of them came to see that either measuring the linear distance across the ponds or finding their perimeter did not necessarily allow them to compare the area of the ponds.

It seemed to me that many now understood that they needed to measure "skating space" on a pond with plane-filling units, which I believed was an essential concept. At the same time, I realized that they were lacking some key information that would help them think about the problem. For instance, they were clearly unaware that there is such a thing as a unit of area. While they knew about rulers and tape measures, and at least *thought* they could use them accurately, they didn't know about square units. In addition, they didn't know the meaning of the words *perimeter* and *area,* so they were making up their own words to describe what they were trying to measure. They often called the area of the pond the "skating space," which at least seemed accurate. The perimeter they called the *edge,* or sometimes the *circumference,* which was a term we had used when measuring pumpkins in the fall. I thought that if I gave them some of the vocabulary now, after they had been thinking about the ideas, it would help them communicate.

For the next lesson I decided we would look specifically at the area and perimeter of some rectangles that could be measured with square-inch tiles. I cut out a set of rectangles, each with an area of 36 square inches. I

65

70

75

80

85

90

would ask partners to find the length and width of the rectangles and then to find the area and perimeter. Before we could start, I needed to do some specific instruction. I also prepared a chart that listed the ideas children had tried in order to find the "skating space" of the ponds.

I began by showing them one of the rectangles, the 9×4. "Today we're going to look at rectangular ponds," I began, "because they're a lot easier to measure. You have all been working so hard to figure out the skating space on our ponds, but it's been really hard because the ponds are such strange shapes. It's easier with rectangles, because your measuring tools will fit better. Let's look at this one. Some kids think that if you measure around the edge of the pond, you can judge the space inside. They have been measuring that with a ruler. Why does a ruler work for that edge?"

One student volunteered that the edge is a line and a ruler can measure a line. "Do we have a word for that edge?" I asked. After several students had offered words like *edge*, *circumference*, and *side*, I told them, "Mathematicians use the word *perimeter*. It's like circumference, but perimeter is the outside edge of any shape, not just a circle. Rulers measure lines, and the perimeter is a line."

I continued, "We haven't found the rulers to be too helpful in comparing the ponds' space for skating. Do we have any other material that would help us measure skating space? What could we use to measure the space covered by this rectangular pond? Keep in mind that a ruler measures lines."

Pat spoke right up: "The tiles, because they're inch by inch." From the very beginning of this activity, Pat had been intent on covering the space in the ponds with equivalent area. He and his partner, Leslie, had tried a variety of things, including square-inch tiles, but they had never been satisfied. However, I felt they had been on a very productive track the whole time, and their efforts were bearing fruit in his clear words.

I acknowledged the usefulness of his idea by telling the class, "Pat is exactly right. Mathematicians use square inches, just like these tiles, to measure area. These are like rulers for the space inside. In fact, there are lots of other units for measuring area. Just as Pat said, these tiles measure 'inch by inch.' The others are similar, but with another measurement. Can you think of any?"

"Centimeters?"

"Millimeters?"

"Feet?"

"Kilometers?"

"Miles?"

Suzanne

GRADE 3, FEBRUARY

I noted that the children knew the names for several linear units. As each unit was volunteered, I responded by talking about the corresponding square unit. For example, I said, "Yes. We use square miles to measure the area of very large spaces, like a state. You see those in the atlas we look at." I similarly identified square centimeters, square millimeters, square feet, and square kilometers.

Next I called attention to the poster that listed children's ideas for measuring area.

"What do you think of these ideas now?" I asked. "Which ones will really help you to compare the area of two ponds? Many of you measured the perimeter of your ponds. Did that tell you how much skating space they had?" I noticed that Nina was nodding yes, while Sergio was emphatically shaking his head no.

Ideas We Have Tried for Measuring Our Ponds

1.   Measure the length and the width with a ruler.
2.   Measure the perimeter with beans, buttons, a tape measure, or cubes.
3.   Cover the space with buttons, tiles, beans, rainbow cubes, or connecting cubes.

Bridget spoke up in her usual clear-thinking way, "Perimeter won't help us. You can have a really big perimeter with lots of jogs and not much area inside."

Joshua, a quiet but very thoughtful student who rarely puts his ideas into words unless he's very sure, added, "Yeah. Perimeter and area are not related. You can have a long perimeter and not much skating space."

"Do you mean they're not ever related, or they're not always related?" I asked.

"Only sometimes," answered Joshua.

"Yeah, sometimes," agreed Bridget.

Mindful that this lesson with rectangles was simply designed to give students the necessary tools to return to their irregularly shaped "ponds," I showed them the set of rectangles I had cut out, had them choose one with a partner, and asked them to pick up rulers and square-inch tiles and set to work. They eagerly went off, appearing to enjoy a task that was much more manageable than the ponds they had been working on.

As I walked around, I noticed that they were measuring and recording carefully and, for the most part, accurately. Some, like Vic, were talking

135

140

145

150

155

160

through the process. They used the new words they had just learned over
and over, with emphasis, as if trying to stick them in their heads. Vic said,
"Now we measured the *length* right here, and it's 12 inches, and then we
measured the *width* right here, and it's three inches. So the *length* is 12 and
the *width* is three. Then we went around the edge, and that's the *perimeter*.
So the *perimeter* is 30 inches. And the *area* is 12 plus 12 plus 12, so it's 12,
24, 36. The *area* is 36 square inches, and the *perimeter* is 30 inches."

As we gathered together in a group and looked at the rectangles, the
children seemed satisfied as well as surprised by some of the findings.
Vic, for instance, was so surprised by the fact that rectangles had different
perimeters and the same area that he didn't believe it. He kept going over
the figures, trying to understand what he was seeing. "Ours has a
perimeter of 30 and an area of 36, but this other one has a perimeter of 40
and still an area of 36. And look at this one. It has a perimeter of 24 and
an area of 36. How can that be?"

"That's ours," said Bridget. "It's right. See, it's a square. The perimeter
is all sixes, so that's 6 + 6 = 12 and 12 + 12 = 24, so it's right. And the area
is 36. We counted the tiles. It's right."

This was an idea that would have to settle in. Vic and his classmates
would need to ponder it for some time. For now, I felt satisfied that my
students had the experience that they needed to go back to their ponds.

CASE 31

Counting cubes in cubes

Bobbie

GRADE 4, SEPTEMBER

Early in the school year, I asked my class to build an object out of cubes,
then determine the number of cubes they had used. I was expecting them
to build multilayered structures, like a throne I had built as an example,
but many of the children built very simple shapes. Even so, when they
counted their cubes, I noticed that most of them were counting by ones

instead of organizing the structures into sections and counting groups. I
decided we should revisit counting cubes in basic multilayered objects.

The next day I presented a cube-building activity. I used a $1 \times 1 \times 1$
cube to introduce the idea of a cube and to talk about dimensions. Then I
asked the class to build a $2 \times 2 \times 2$ cube. Several children built shapes that
were 2 units in each dimension, but were not in fact cubes.

When I asked the class what a $2 \times 2 \times 2$ cube would look like, some
children insisted that it had to be a square on all faces. The other children
were quick to catch on. They were able to count fairly quickly that there
were 8 cubes in a $2 \times 2 \times 2$ cube structure; there were no hidden cubes.

Encouraged by their success, the children next went on to make a
$3 \times 3 \times 3$ cube. This is where it got interesting. The construction of this
cube resulted in a hidden cube inside, and I wondered how my students
would handle counting the smaller cubes in a $3 \times 3 \times 3$.

As they worked diligently building their cubes, some more adeptly
than others, they all seemed to have the idea of what a $3 \times 3 \times 3$ cube
should look like. When they had finished, I asked them to count how
many cubes they had used in their construction.

STEVEN: [*looking puzzled*] I think there's 12.

BILLY: I counted 9 on one side and multiplied that by 3, and got 27.
            There's 9 on one side [*pointing to a face*], and you multiply
            that 3 times.

ASHLEY: I came up with 27. I counted by threes and added them up.

SOPHIA: I counted by ones and got 27. I had to open up the middle.

CHRISTINE: I got 54.

I asked Christine to show me how she got 54, and she began to count
each square on each face.

Jamie had used a similar strategy. When you added the 9 individual
squares on each face of the $3 \times 3 \times 3$ cube, they added up to 54. These

children weren't recognizing that their strategy was faulty, or that they had neglected to count the middle cube and were counting some cubes twice and even three times. Christine muttered that she felt it wasn't right, but she wasn't quite sure why not.

I held up a $3 \times 3 \times 3$ cube and asked the class if counting each square on each side would be an accurate strategy. The class was quiet for a few moments; then a few hands shot up. Brenda rather emphatically insisted that it wouldn't work. She protested that you would end up counting some cubes twice and end up double the amount. Indeed, 54, the number of square units showing on the $3 \times 3 \times 3$ cube, is double 27, the count of its volume. Some children seemed to be contemplating what Brenda had said. I could see some heads nodding; others looked puzzled; and a few looked indifferent. Just then the recess bell rang, and it was time to stop.

Reflecting upon that math session, I realize that the children shared an incredible amount of information with me. Initially I had not intended this activity to be focused on surface area and volume, yet these issues came up in the process of their counting. How do children come to envision the cubes that compose a shape and see that they're not necessarily the same as the squares we see on the surface? What do they need to understand about surface area and volume in order to distinguish one from the other? What helps us know when there are objects to count that we cannot see?

The children's confusions have caused me to reflect further upon *my* understandings about surface area and volume, and I feel the ideas are still somewhat fuzzy in my own head. Brenda pointed out that when you count the squares for surface area, some cubes are counted twice, and you end up with double the number of cubes in the structure. Does it always work out that way? I think not! When I look at the $2 \times 2 \times 2$ cube, I see that the volume is 8 but there are 24 squares showing on the surface area, and $8 \times 3 = 24$. With a unit cube, the volume is 1 and the surface area is 6: $1 \times 6 = 6$. I wonder what happens with a $4 \times 4 \times 4$, or a $5 \times 5 \times 5$. Will I find a pattern?

Growing towers

Lucy

My class had just finished some work with area. Their tools for exploring area were paper squares and triangles, computer software, and geoboards. On the geoboards, they challenged themselves to create weird-shaped designs and then tried to figure out the area. They really enjoyed both creating the designs and figuring out how to measure them. When they couldn't figure out a particular design, some tried to figure out what they needed to change so that they could determine the area. There was much animated conversation in the small groups as children worked and talked about their thinking.

Since my students were so interested in area, I wanted to see if I could take this further. In some material from NCTM, I had found an activity that sounded interesting: Students were looking at the surface area of a stack of cubes and making predictions about how the surface area changed when new cubes were added. I wondered what my students would think about area as it related to a three-dimensional figure.

LESSON ONE

I gathered a small group of four children and began by explaining that we were going to look at a kind of area called "surface area." I compared it to thinking about wrapping something with paper. I had given them each some cubes stacked in towers of two, and we started there.

SARAH: You need to know the area of the wrapping paper. You need to know the whole area. Like the inside?

RON: What?

I, too, wondered what she meant.

SARAH:	[*picking up the cubes and looking at them*] You just need to know the outside.	
TEACHER:	So if you're going to pay attention to all sides of this shape, what is the surface area of the whole thing?	
MOIRA:	Like this? Do you mean this side, all the sides?	280
TEACHER:	Yes, all the sides, as if you were going to wrap it in paper.	
MOIRA:	Are we counting these two blocks?	
SARAH:	Do we count just the top?	
TEACHER:	All sides. The surface.	
MOIRA:	Like, so, 1, 2, 3, 4, 5, 6, 7, 8. [*She points to and counts each of the square units on the vertical faces of the two cubes.*]	285
JEFF:	No. Actually it is 4. See 1, 2, 3, 4. [*Jeff also points to the four vertical faces, but he counts both square units as one.*]	
MOIRA:	It's 10.	
TEACHER:	I heard Jeff say it was 4, but Moira said it was 8, then 10.	290
RON:	[*pointing to a face of the tower, counting each square unit*] This is 2—1, 2.	
SARAH:	I think it is 1.	
TEACHER:	What is the surface area of one cube?	
RON:	[*touching all faces of a single cube*] It would be like 1, 2, 3, 4, 5, 6.	295
JEFF:	Actually, it depends on…	
MOIRA:	I don't get it.	
TEACHER:	So I'm asking, can the surface area of one cube be the same as the surface area of the two-cube tower? If I wanted to know how much paper I needed to cover both of these—if I had enough paper to cover one cube, would it cover two?	300
SARAH:	Hmmmm!	

TEACHER:	Do they have the same surface area? [*The children shook their heads no.*] So, surface area means all the sides. And we're counting one square as our unit of measure [*pointing to a face of one cube*]. One square is one unit of area.
RON:	1, 2, 3, 4, 5, 6.
MOIRA:	10.
TEACHER:	I hear 10 and 6.
MOIRA:	With one cube it is 6; two cubes is 10.
JEFF:	If you count the bottom, it's 10; if you don't, it's 9.
TEACHER:	I hear 6, 10, and Jeff is talking about the bottom.
MOIRA:	You're not supposed to count this part. [*She pulls apart the two cubes and points to the top and bottom attached faces.*] So that's not a side when they're together. That would be 10.
SARAH:	Yeah, 10.

Everyone was talking at once, more to themselves than to me or the group.

SARAH:	But there are two cubes, so that means there would have to be 12. [*She is remembering that one cube has 6 square units.*]
TEACHER:	Sarah says that because there are two cubes and one cube has 6, then two cubes must be 12.
MOIRA:	But this part is stuck together, so this part doesn't count. [*She pulls the cubes apart and points to the two hidden square units.*]
SARAH:	Oh, so the bottom of this and the top of this don't count.
JEFF:	The top one of this [bottom cube] and the bottom one of this [top cube] don't count.

Now all four children agreed that the surface area of the two-cube tower was 10 units. I also noticed they were counting the sides in different ways: some going around the individual cubes one at a time, some counting one face of the tower at a time.

TEACHER: How were you keeping track of what you were counting?

Sarah described wrapping around the four sides of one cube and the top, then the four sides of the other cube and then the bottom. Ron said he did 2, 4, 6, 8 (counting each vertical face), then the top and bottom.

Now that the children were more sure of what we were counting—that the surface area of a single cube is 6 square units and the surface area of the two-cube tower is 10—I thought we could move on.

TEACHER: Now let's add one cube to your tower. What is the surface area now?

Each child added a cube to make a tower of three cubes. Sarah suggested, "10 plus another 5," while the others offered 13, 14, and 15.

TEACHER: I hear people saying 13, 14, and 15.

JEFF: The top of the two [the original stack of two cubes] is taken away.

MOIRA: So it's 14.

SARAH: It's 13, because you have to take away the bottom of this one too. So it must be 13.

As the children spoke, they kept turning their towers round and round, counting square units. I was intrigued by how much they needed to think about this, to actually count the squares over and over.

JEFF: There's 14. [*He counts down each of the three square units on each face.*] 1, 2, 3, [*turn*] 4, 5, 6, [*turn*] 7, 8, 9, [*turn*] 10, 11, 12, [*and then touching the top and bottom*] 13, 14.

MOIRA: 6 + 6 is 12. Then add 2 more is 14.

SARAH: This one is 9… so 14. The middle cube doesn't have either the top or the bottom, so it's just 4. But this one [the top cube] is 5 and so is the bottom one, it's 5. So it must be 14. So instead of 10 plus 5, it's 10 plus 4.

TEACHER: Who can tell me in your own words what Sarah just said?

MOIRA: There's two 5s, and this one is only 4, because the other two are blocking it.

TEACHER: So this end cube gives 5 units of surface area, 4 plus 1, that's 5 + 5. The middle one only has 4.

SARAH: That one doesn't have more because there is no top or bottom on it.

I now gave the children a piece of paper to record their work and asked them to keep track of the number of cubes and the surface area of each of their towers. They recorded on a chart like this:

Number of cubes	Surface area
1	6
2	10
3	14

MOIRA: How many do you add? You add 4 to each one. So the next one would be 18.

TEACHER: Do you think so?

RON: Yeah, it would be 18 because these two would be 8 [*pointing to the two middle cubes*], and then 5 and 5, so 18.

MOIRA: No, it wouldn't. I need another. [*She grabs a cube and starts counting.*] Oh yeah, 18, because each time you add 4.

RON: Like Sarah said, these two [the middle cubes] are 4 [each], and 5 plus 5.

MOIRA: Because 6 + 4 is 10, 10 add 4 is 14, and 4 is 18. You're adding 4 each time a cube is added.

TEACHER: Why are you adding 4?

MOIRA: Because you take away this top part and another one, so you're just adding 4.

RON: Yeah, 4.

TEACHER: So where are the 4 you're adding every time?

RON: In the middle, in one cube.

TEACHER: Can you show us what you mean, Moira?

MOIRA: You take away this top and this bottom. Well, you take away
            this bottom [*pointing to the square unit covered by the next cube*]   390
            and you add this one, which gives you a different bottom.
            But it's still a bottom. And it's, um, you're just adding 4.
            Because 5 + 5 is 10, 10 plus 4 is 14. [*She points to an end cube
            for 5 square units and the other end cube for another 5 square
            units, plus the 4 square units from the middle cube.*]   395

SARAH: So can we write it down?

The children kept adding cubes to their stacks and recording the
numbers on the chart. First they wrote the number of cubes and added 4
to the previous number for the surface area, then added a cube to the
stack and checked the total.   400

TEACHER: So, Moira and Sarah think they've made a rule here, that
            every time you add a cube, you add on a surface area of 4.

Moira read off her chart: 6, 10, 14, 18.

TEACHER: [*turning to the boys*] Do you agree that every time you add on
            a cube, you add on 4 to the surface area? Can you explain   405
            why? Does that make sense?

Jeff held a stack of five cubes. He then showed the group how he was
counting all the square units on each face of the tower—5 + 5 + 5 + 5 + 2.
He pointed to the 5 square units on each of the four vertical faces, then
added the 2 for the ends. But then he showed us that it was also 4 + 4 + 4   410
+ 4 + 4 + 2 if he counted around all the square units of each cube in the
tower and then added the ends. He said it was $(4 \times 5) + 2$ and $(5 \times 4) + 2$.
The others agreed. Pretty good, I thought.

It was almost time to end, but I built a $2 \times 2 \times 2$ cube and asked what
they thought the surface area would be. Their eyes grew big. They were   415
very interested. With only a few minutes to work, we didn't do much, but
they were very excited. They wanted to find out how that shape would
work. They were thinking about patterns and wondering what the
relationships would be when other 2×2 layers were added on.

Later I thought about what had happened with these four students. I was interested that Moira was quick to notice, from the data on her chart, that the difference was 4. But they all still needed to count and really think about it. Did it really work every time? Why was it happening? They had to think about whether they needed to add on 4, 5, or 6 square units for each additional cube. It took them a while to puzzle through what happened to the tops and bottoms each time a cube was added. I was intrigued by their interest.

LESSON TWO

A few days later, I continued our work on surface area, bringing Thomas and Chris into the original small group. Remembering how intrigued the children had been with the idea of a $2 \times 2 \times 2$ tower, I began the lesson there.

Within a few minutes, they figured out that the surface area would be 24. Some looked at six faces with four units each. Ron counted the units on one layer of cubes—2, 4, 6, 8, plus the 4 on the bottom make 12—and then added the two layers together. Chris thought of it as $4 + 4 = 8$; $2 \times 8 = 16$; $16 + 8$ for the top and bottom faces, and got 24.

When I asked about adding another layer, most thought that the surface area would increase by 12. But when they actually added a third layer and counted, it was easy for them to see that the increase was only 8 since the top faces were "not really new ones" to count. As Ron said, "We'd already counted them before."

THOMAS: The top is just moving up; it is always the same top, and the bottom [of the new layer] isn't there anymore.

SARAH: It was the same thing that happened last time [with the towers of single cubes].

CHRIS: It's just 8 more; you just count around the sides.

Once everyone was satisfied that they'd found the pattern, I decided to introduce a new idea.

TEACHER: What happens to the surface area when you pull off one cube?

420

425

430

435

440

445

450

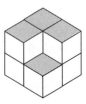 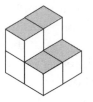

One cube removed   Two cubes removed

MOIRA: It stays the same.

RON: Yeah, because you took off three...

SARAH: But you add three, because of three showing inside.

TEACHER: Will that happen anywhere? Can you take off any cube and it would always stay the same?

RON: Yes, if I take any one off, it's the same.

TEACHER: What will happen if you take off two cubes?

RON: It will be the same.

SARAH: No, it wouldn't be the same.

MOIRA: Because you're losing two. I still have these two and these two [*pointing to the newly exposed faces and the corresponding faces of the cube taken away*], but the two end ones are gone.

Time was almost up, but I asked what would happen if cubes were removed from a $3 \times 3 \times 3$ block.

RON: It will stay the same.

TEACHER: So if we take any cubes off, the surface area will stay the same?

SARAH: Wait, it won't be the same if you take it off from the middle.

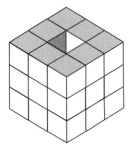

Measuring Space in One, Two, and Three Dimensions

THOMAS: It will be a higher number.

RON: No, it will be the same.... No, it will be one more actually, because of the bottom.

470

MOIRA: No, it will be five more.

TEACHER: Where is that five coming from?

MOIRA: If you take that cube out, there's 4 plus 1 is 5 more.

THOMAS: No, it's only 4. Because the top one inside is the same as the top one on the one we already counted. Because we replaced it.

475

SARAH: That makes sense.

LESSON THREE

On another day, I set Jeff and Ron to work on another surface-area problem. I gave them four cubes of different sizes—with edges of 1, 2, 3, and 4 units—and asked what they thought the surface area of each would be. The boys recorded the surface areas as 6, 24, 54, and 96—and Jeff declared the next one would be 150, though I hadn't made one that size.

480

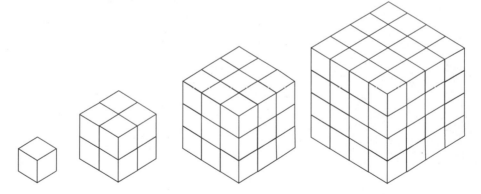

I asked if they could state a rule to describe how the areas were changing. I reminded them how they had made their first rule by looking at how the numbers had grown when they worked with the first towers, adding four square units for each cube.

485

First Jeff said the areas were all 3-numbers (multiples of 3). Ron said they were also count-by-6-numbers. Then he said the areas were always six times one face of the whole cube.

490

Ron suggested that we were adding 3 sixes every time. He was noticing the distance between 6 and 24, or 18. He guessed the same was true for 24 to 54, but when he realized that distance was 30, Jeff pointed out that was 5 sixes. They figured out it was 7 sixes between 54 and 96, and observed a pattern: 3, 5, 7. So Jeff said he thought it must be 9 sixes to 150!

495

I was amazed at these nine-year-olds. I wanted to dig right in myself and figure out where the pattern was coming from. Writing things down, I saw there really was a pattern of 1, 3, 5, ... if you start with a $0 \times 0 \times 0$ cube, giving an increase of 2 sixes in the difference each time. But I haven't worked any more on it.

500

Cube dimensions	Surface area	Difference
$0 \times 0 \times 0$	0	
		$6 = 6 \times 1$
$1 \times 1 \times 1$	6	
		$18 = 6 \times 3$
$2 \times 2 \times 2$	24	
		$30 = 6 \times 5$
$3 \times 3 \times 3$	54	
		$42 = 6 \times 7$
$4 \times 4 \times 4$	96	
		$54 = 6 \times 9$
$5 \times 5 \times 5$	150	

C H A P T E R

8

Highlights of related research

by Kristine Reed Woleck

WALLY: The big rug is the giant's castle. The small one is Jack's house.

EDDIE: Both rugs are the same.

WALLY: They can't be the same. Watch me. I'll walk around the rug. Now watch—walk, walk, walk, walk, walk, walk, walk, walk, walk—count all these walks. Okay. Now count the other rug. Walk, walk, walk, walk, walk. See? That one has more walks.

EDDIE: No fair. You cheated. You walked faster.

WALLY: I don't have to walk. I can just look.

EDDIE:	I can look too. But you have to measure it. You need a ruler. About six hundred inches or feet.
WALLY:	We have a ruler.
EDDIE:	Not that one. Not the short kind. You have to use the long kind that gets curled up in a box.
WALLY:	Use people. People's bodies. Lying down in a row.
EDDIE:	That's a great idea. I never even thought of that.

—from *Wally's Stories,* Vivian Gussin Paley
(Harvard University Press, 1981)

These five-year-olds are just beginning the journey into measurement that will lead them, year by year, to more sophisticated connections between their spatial sense and number. Measurement is a strand of mathematics with many practical applications in everyday life; it is mathematical work grounded in concrete experiences. How tall am I? Is this piece of wood long enough? Which box will hold more? Measurement may seem quite simple on the surface, but it encompasses many truly complex concepts and understandings. Educational research reminds us of this hidden complexity.

The research findings cited in this essay serve as a lens through which we can revisit the classrooms described in the casebook and view the issues children confront as they develop concepts of measurement. Connecting research to the classroom can be a powerful tool for us as teachers, as observers, and as learners, opening our eyes to the big ideas—and, as in Wally's case, the "great ideas"—that children encounter with each step of their journey toward learning to measure one, two, and three dimensions of space.

What is big? What is small?

Measurement of space is the intersection of spatial reasoning and number sense. Children must first identify and understand what aspect of an object they are going to measure. Are they to measure its length? its area? its volume? Once they have determined this, children can go on to make direct and indirect comparisons as they undertake their measurement work.

Measurement terms like *big* and *tall* are heard frequently every day. Children bring with them to any measuring task their previous encounters with this informal, everyday use of the language of measurement, and these previous encounters undoubtedly influence their ideas about measurement (Bishop, 1983). Initially, as children attempt to define what is meant by *big, tall,* and the like, their language speaks to an overall impression of size. Kindergartners' comments in Barbara's case 12 and Beverly's case 5 are filled with such statements as these:

"Super big! Very very big big."

"The box is big like a tree."

"That one is longer. That one is taller."

These statements reflect children's initial awareness of a measurable property of an object (Schwartz, 1995). During the elementary grades, children's ideas of measurement progress from a qualitative perception of a measurable attribute to a more quantitative description, and ultimately to a numeric comparison between some object and a specific unit.

We can measure many different, specific aspects of an object, including height, width, area, and volume. In Mary's case 1, the children describe a variety of measurements for a puddle, including how deep it is and how far it is around. To measure anything meaningfully, children must know what attribute of an object they are measuring and be able to select a unit appropriate to that attribute. Length is measurement requiring one-dimensional units; area, two-dimensional; and volume, three-dimensional. Differentiating between these measurements can be challenging for children. For example, Lehrer, Jenkins, and Osana (1998) found that some young children measured the area of a square by measuring the length of

5

10

15

20

25

the square with a ruler, sliding the ruler down a bit, measuring the length between the two sides, sliding the ruler down a bit more, measuring the length between the sides again, and so on. These children treated length as a space-filling attribute. Similarly, the work of others in the field indicates that children often look at only one dimension and fail to recognize that, unlike length, area is a plane-filling attribute, a covering up of a region of space (Nitabach & Lehrer, 1996; Wilson & Rowland, 1993).

Measurement may be defined as a comparison—either qualitative or quantitative—of a given aspect of two or more objects. The point of reference is significant in a comparison, particularly in the case of qualities such as "tall" or "short" that are not absolute. A seven-year-old may be tall in comparison to a four-year-old, but short in comparison to a sixteen-year-old. The unit used as a point of reference in a quantitative comparison is significant as well; a girl could measure 5 *feet* tall or 60 *inches* tall. In addition, some comparisons of size are not well-defined. For instance, determining how "big" an object is could reasonably be interpreted to refer to any of several aspects of the object—its height, its volume, and so forth. In Olivia's case 4, children are asked to compare rectangles and determine which is the biggest. Initially, they base their comparisons on the most conspicuous perceptual cue—the length of the rectangles. On another day, when the children cover the rectangles with tiles, the experience carries them beyond their original perception of "bigness" and reveals another way in which they could compare and order the rectangles.

Direct comparison sets the foundation for measurement work. It is number-free and so focuses attention on the attribute being measured (Clements & Battista, 1986; Schwartz, 1995; Wilson & Rowland, 1993). For direct comparison, children physically place two objects side by side or on top of one another to determine their size relationship. They develop concepts such as "longer than" and "shorter than" from direct comparisons, as when a young child exclaims in the block area, "My castle is as tall as the block shelf!" or when Barbara's kindergartners (case 12) spontaneously compare the intriguing shipping box in their classroom to their own bodies. Barbara's kindergartners do not yet know enough about units to make a quantitative measurement.

Measurement experiences in the classroom typically build from direct to indirect comparisons, and much literature in the field supports this progression (Clements & Battista, 1986; Schwartz, 1995; Wilson & Rowland, 1993). In all dimensions of space, indirect comparison requires the use of some intermediate material; this could be a nonstandard manipulative or a conventional tool. In Rosemarie's case 6, children compare containers by filling them with beans, sand, and water. This illustrates an indirect comparison of capacity. Another common example of indirect comparison is the use of a piece of string to compare the height, width, or perimeter of two objects. Often, young children use their own bodies as a referent for making indirect comparisons (Carpenter, 1976). We see this when kindergartners compare two block towers by marking the height of each tower on their chest with the side of a hand.

When children make an indirect comparison using multiple copies of a nonstandard or standard unit (e.g., many buttons or many inch-squares), measurement moves from comparison in a general sense to a comparison that can be quantified by counting the units. Because geometric measurement involves a continuous property of space such as length, area, or volume, the counting of units calls for a process known as spatial structuring. Through spatial structuring, the children break down and organize a space, either physically or mentally, into parts they can quantify or units they can count (Battista, 1998; Wilson & Rowland, 1993). In this essay's later sections, we will delve more deeply into the big ideas just mentioned—spatial structuring and units—as well as other measurement concepts that transcend all dimensions of space.

Some developmental research asserts that all measurement learning occurs in conjunction with the child's development of premeasurement concepts, the most fundamental being conservation. When children recognize that an object's change of position in space or its division into parts does not change its overall size, they are said to conserve (Wilson & Rowland, 1993). Piaget articulated stages of measurement development linked to the development of conservation (Piaget & Inhelder, 1967; Carpenter, 1976; Copeland, 1984). Though Piaget's work can continue to serve as a guide, some research indicates that the link between conservation and measurement concepts is not as strong as once thought (Hiebert, 1981). Children who do not yet conserve can still benefit from concrete measurement experiences; even if they do not yet conserve, they can learn to compare two objects indirectly, make use of units, and understand that having an equal number of units implies that two objects have equal measures (Hiebert, 1984). What's more, while Piaget's work takes the perspective of individual development, it appears that social context—interactions and discussions with peers as they undertake concrete measurement experiences—can influence and support children's development of measurement concepts (McClain, Cobb, Gravemeijer, & Estes, 1999).

From parts to whole (and back again)

Decomposing and recomposing space is critical to the measurement process, whether we are comparing space without numbers or quantifying the space numerically. Children's development of part-whole relations plays a fundamental role in their work to decompose and recompose space.

In Andrea's case 7, "Perplexing Walls," second graders attempt to draw their oddly-shaped classroom from a bird's-eye perspective. Some of these children move around the room and identify familiar shapes in the space. Some use yardsticks or pencils to judge the angles of the walls. Some simply draw a rectangle and struggle to determine where doors or windows should be placed. The measurement occurring in this "Perplexing Walls" case may not be obvious at first glance. The episode seems to have a different flavor than the cases in which children compare boxes, count color tiles, or use tape measures. What is significant about the work of Andrea's second graders, and how does it relate to concepts of measurement?

Andrea's students decompose and recompose space. To varying degrees, they see the whole shape of their classroom, and they attempt to make sense of this whole by breaking it down into its parts—the geometric shapes they see embedded within the whole. Andrea writes:

> Nadia saw that the classroom could be divided into yet another rectangle, with a line running the full width of our classroom. Nora saw that Nadia's dividing line, crossing Susannah's and Jack's, created several smaller rectangles, which, when combined, created her larger rectangle. Thomas bounced up and down in his seat as he declared that the cubby area could be considered a rectangle as well. Finally, we examined the area created by the diagonal wall. A near universal cry went up, "It's a triangle!" (pp. 43–44)

While Andrea's students see a whole space composed of many different geometric shapes, decomposing can also mean being able to see a whole composed of identical parts or units. The very act of decomposing space into units is the basis of measurement in one, two, and three dimensions. As children impose a mental structure on the space they are measuring (discussed in detail in section 4 of this essay), they decompose and recompose space in an organized way. This allows them to arrive at a count of the units that fill the measured space.

Experiences with decomposing and recomposing space are related to a child's development of conservation. Through such experiences, children come to understand that some transformations of length, area, and volume, such as cutting and rearranging parts, may change the appearance of the space, but the total measure—the sum of the parts—remains unchanged (Van de Walle, 1998; Lehrer, in press). As we will see in section 6, decomposing and recomposing space also serves as the foundation for measurement formulas.

The development of part-whole relations is essential for work in decomposing and recomposing space. Children who recognize part-whole relations can see the whole of an object, quantity, or space, as well as its component parts; they are also able to coordinate the parts with the whole. Some of Andrea's students are able to find familiar shapes within the whole classroom space and can readily coordinate these shapes with the whole. However, for other children in Andrea's class, this coordination of the parts and whole is more difficult. Will and Evan, for instance, identify a component part—the rectangular shape they see as the cubbies—but they are unable to coordinate this part with the other shapes of the classroom space, and so they draw it as a separate shape on their paper, unconnected to the rest of their drawing.

While Andrea's "Perplexing Walls" case is concerned with the decomposition and recomposition of two-dimensional space, this strategy can be applied to measurement in other dimensions as well. For instance, to measure a crooked line, we can break the line into a series of straight segments; the sum of these parts equals the total length. To some extent, Will and Evan are doing this linear decomposing in Andrea's second case (case 8), when they decompose the perimeter of the classroom wall by wall and note the straight lines that come together to make corners.

Josie's case 10 provides evidence of decomposing in three-dimensional space; there she describes the children's strategies for visualizing and building a structure of interlocking cubes. For example, Cassie sees the structure in chunks: "two across the top, two going down, then two going across again, but at the bottom" (p. 56). By decomposing the three-dimensional structure, Cassie is able to visualize and recompose the whole.

At times, children use a decomposing and recomposing strategy to compare regions of space without attaching numerical values. We see this strategy in Maura's case 20, as Keith uses an overlay-and-cutting technique to compare the space in two paper gardens, one a rectangle and the other a square. Keith cuts out the two shapes, lays the square on top of the rectangle, cuts the "extra" off the side of the square, and leaves the extra top piece of the rectangle. He then places the extra strip from the square across the top, showing that the extra from the square is bigger than the extra piece of the rectangle.

He concludes that the square is bigger than the rectangle. The concrete, physical nature of Keith's work is noteworthy; as children develop their ability to decompose and recompose space, they need many opportunities to physically cut, manipulate, and rearrange the space and reflect on these actions (Nitabach & Lehrer, 1996).

Sometimes, children decompose and recompose space to determine quantitative measures, as when they use the measurement of a known region to determine the measurement of an unknown region (Lehrer, in press). In Rachel's case 23, for instance, Claire explains how the area of a triangle that is embedded within a 3×4 rectangle can be quantified:

> "Brit got the right answer, because all together there's 12 squares, and… the triangle is half of this rectangle. Half of 12 equals 6." (p. 126)

As she decomposes and recomposes space here, Claire uses a known region (the rectangle) to determine the measure of an unknown region (the triangle). This strategy allows her to assign numerical values to the space. What's more, her use of quantitative measurements involves concepts of unit, concepts that we will examine further in the next section of this essay.

Understanding units

Identifying a unit and finding the number of those units that occupy a given space is fundamental to measurement. The concept of unit and unit iteration, however, is quite complex and presents a variety of issues for children to confront. Teachers can foster understanding by offering experiences with both nonstandard and standard units of measure.

Measurement, in the conventional sense of the term, involves the same basic process in all three dimensions of space. That is, we select an appropriate unit for the attribute being measured, compare the unit to the object, and then report the number of units that fit in the structured space (Rowan & Lindquist, 1989). Clearly, an understanding of *unit* is key.

The child's understanding of unit begins with the realization that we must select a unit related to the particular aspect of the object we are measuring (Wilson & Rowland, 1993). Thus, to measure length, we must use a linear unit; to measure area, a unit that has a two-dimensional, plane-filling property; to measure volume, a three-dimensional unit. The notion of using a plane-filling unit for area is particularly challenging for children; we can see this in the work of Ellie and other students in Lydia's third-grade class (case 21) when they are asked to measure the area of their hands. Many of the children choose a tape measure and focus on the linear dimensions of their hands rather than selecting a tool, such as tiles, that they could use to cover their hands and arrive at an area measure. These children do not yet recognize the need for a plane-filling unit and so simply use linear units to measure area. Lehrer (in press) also describes a "resemblance bias" in which children tend to select area units of the same shape as the area they are measuring—for instance, triangles to measure the area of a triangle, or, as Lydia describes in case 21, trapezoids to measure trapezoids.

Once we have selected an appropriate unit, unit iteration can begin. Iteration entails using a unit to subdivide a space and counting these subdivisions. Here again, we see the significance of part-whole relations and spatial structuring. Depending on which aspect is being measured, units are laid end-to-end (one dimension), tiled to cover an area (two dimensions), or packed to fill a space (three dimensions). Children can use connecting cubes, rulers, and other standard and nonstandard measuring tools to physically embody the unit. By using multiple copies of these tools, children concretize the repetition of multiple units in a series, as when Adam (in Josie's case 16) tapes metersticks together to measure the distance from the floor to the ceiling. As children develop a more abstract sense of iteration, they will reposition a single measurement tool end-over-end to repeat the unit (Clements & Battista, 1986; Thompson & Van de Walle, 1985). Bonnie, in Mabel's case 15, steps toward this understanding of iteration when she demonstrates "putting down one ruler, then a second, then moving the first to the place after the second, and so on" (p. 78).

When children begin to segment and quantify space with repeated units, they must recognize several principles. For one, the iterated unit must be a constant size. Because children have a tendency to mix units, they need many real-world measurement experiences over time to discover for themselves the importance of using identical units. Some research reports that by the end of the elementary grades, most students understand the need for identical units for length but not for area measure (Lehrer, in press).

Children must also recognize that, in measuring any dimension, the units must match up with the beginning and end of the object or space being measured, and there can be no gaps or overlaps. Furthermore, units placed end-to-end to measure a linear attribute must be placed parallel to the measured object. Children tend to honor the boundaries of a space and take much care to keep their units from extending "outside the lines" when measuring, but they often pay no attention to the cracks they are leaving between units as they lay them down or fill a space (Nitabach & Lehrer, 1996).

Segmenting a space with units sometimes requires dealing with fractions of those units—what children may call "leftovers." We see this in Lydia's case 21, when her students are measuring the area of their hands; those who have traced their hands on a grid tackle parts of units by combining partial squares to create whole units.

Over time, as children use a variety of units in concrete measurement activities, they can discover that the numeric measure of an object or space depends on the particular unit used (Clements & Battista, 2001). This requires that children reason about and reflect on why they arrive at different counts when using different units. The understanding that the numeric measure is dependent on the unit used is further refined with time, hands-on measurement experiences, and opportunities to reflect on those experiences. Over time, children come to recognize that when they use smaller units, more of these units are needed. They also come to see that if the same object is measured on different occasions and the same count results each time, then the same units were used each time.

In Hiebert's research (1981), first graders were shown a crooked road constructed from seven-centimeter rods and were then asked to use five-centimeter rods to build a straight road that would be "just as far to walk" (see Figure 35).

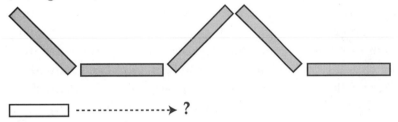

Figure 35 How many shorter rods will make a straight road as long as the crooked one?

Because the children were given shorter rods, they could not simply count to arrive at the solution, and because the given road was crooked, they could not just match the rods. The only way to solve the problem successfully was to recognize that more of the shorter rods would be needed to make a straight road of the same length. The researchers accepted any solution that indicated a greater number of the shorter rods. Many of the children failed this task because they simply laid down the same number of shorter rods, ignoring the difference in size. The children had a tendency to attend to only one feature of the measurement work. In fact, the need to attend to and coordinate multiple features of the measurement work is what renders the inverse relationship between the size and number of units so complex.

We see two very different levels of understanding of this relationship in Rosemarie's case 13. Courtney and Miriam, both first graders, discuss the varying number of foot-lengths different children got when measuring the distance across a doorway.

COURTNEY: I just looked at the numbers, and Miriam has the highest number of foot-lengths, so I think her foot is the biggest.

MIRIAM: I think Gita has the biggest foot because it took fewer of her foot-lengths to measure the doorway. The smaller your foot is, the more feet you need to measure something. (p. 69)

Courtney, typical of children her age, focuses on only one feature of the measurement; in her mind, bigger units should yield higher counts. In contrast, Miriam gives attention not only to the number of units used, but also to the size of the unit used; she has begun to develop an understanding of the way in which the choice of unit affects the count of the units.

As children work to develop the concepts of unit, they can benefit from experiences with both nonstandard units (hands, paces, buttons, acorns) and standard units (inches, centimeters, feet, meters). Such nonstandard units as paper clips are concrete units that can be manipulated individually; they allow children to gradually develop accurate measurement procedures, such as placing units in a series without leaving spaces between them. But, some standard units are also constructed as individual units for a child to manipulate (for example, one-inch tiles) and so can serve this same purpose. The critical element is not so much whether the unit is standard or nonstandard, but rather how children use it. In fact, recent research cautions that with both nonstandard and standard units, misconceptions may arise if children fail to attend to the structure of the space being measured or to the fact that there must be no overlaps or gaps between units (Outhred & McPhail, 2000).

Though most curricula progress systematically from nonstandard to standard units through the early childhood and early elementary years, some evidence that is now emerging challenges this teaching sequence and suggests that children can benefit from earlier work with standard units and even conventional tools (Clements, 1999). In one study, six- to eight-year-old children communicated over the telephone about the length of a line segment drawn on a piece of paper. Centimeter rulers were provided as one tool for this work. Though other research (to be discussed in a later section of this essay) documents children's difficulty with reading rulers, the standard units arranged on the ruler were not problematic for the children in this study (Nunes, Light, & Mason, 1993).

The research cited in the previous paragraph suggests that teachers allow a more fluid movement between nonstandard and standard units in the classroom. Children are aware of standard units from a young age.

They hear references to standard units and standard measuring tools almost daily, and the real-world applications of standard units often make their use more appealing to young children. However, this research and discussion is not to deny the value of nonstandard units in classroom work; nor is it a justification to use only standard units. When children investigate measurement in real-life problem-solving endeavors with both standard and nonstandard units, they gain insights into the problematic nature of nonstandard units (such as handspans) that vary from person to person, and they discover the advantage of standard units in communicating measurements to others (Schwartz, 1995).

Giving structure to space

If children are to accurately count the units of a given space when measuring, they must be able to mentally organize the space in a structured manner. For linear measurement, they must give attention to the two endpoints and then break into parts the distance between the two. For two-dimensional measurement, they must learn to consider more than one dimension at a time. For three-dimensional measurement, children not only must consider more than one dimension at a time, but also must integrate the front, side, and top views of a three-dimensional object in order to see the whole in an organized and accurate way.

Measuring an object or space involves organizing and then quantifying a set of units. To accomplish this, children must impose a mental structure on the space in question. The process of mentally organizing a measurable space by identifying its component units and how they are spatially related is termed *spatial structuring* (Battista, 1998). Though it works differently in one, two, and three dimensions of space, spatial structuring is part of all measurement.

For linear measure, spatial structuring involves mentally organizing the measured distance so that we see a count of linear units that begins at one point (the origin) and continues consistently to another point (the endpoint). When children begin to structure length, their strategies may first include drawing visible hash marks or lines to partition the length into these units. As their measurement sense grows, they come to internalize a unit of length and are able to mentally move along and segment a longer length without making visible marks or lines (Clements & Battista, 2001). This ability to internalize a linear unit and mentally segment a given length into units is a powerful tool children can use for estimating a linear measure, such as how many feet long a bulletin board is.

Spatial structuring in the measurement of area requires that children progress from simply covering a region of space to seeing the underlying array structure—the rows and columns—that coordinates the two dimensions. To determine how children develop an ability to see the array, Battista, Clements, Arnoff, Battista, and Burrow (1998) conducted research in which children used tiles to cover rectangular regions, determined counts of partially drawn arrays, and were asked to draw arrays themselves. This research revealed that, though the array structure may be obvious to an adult, seeing the array requires significant cognitive work for a child. It first entails a recognition of equivalent groups (Battista et al., 1998). As Georgia (in her case 19) asks Kalil to make equal piles of square tiles, she is stepping back to help Kalil establish this notion of equal groups. These equal groups are significant because they are the composite units that can be used to structure a given space. A composite unit, such as a row or column in a rectangular array, is formed from a set of the units that fill a given space; the set as a whole is treated as one composite unit (Battista, 1999). To mentally organize the array structure for measurement of area, children must construct each row or column as a composite unit in and of itself. At the same time, they must iterate and coordinate these rows and columns to form the two-dimensional space as a whole (Battista, 1999; Reynolds & Wheatley, 1996). Once children structure and interpret an array's rows and columns as composite units, they can begin to apply multiplication or repeated addition to quantify a given area, just as Leah does in Maura's case 20.

Leah laid tiles down along the top and the left side of the square.

TEACHER: So how will you count these?

LEAH: There's 6 along the top, and 6 down the side, so that means it's 6 sixes, and that's... [*she thinks for a moment*] 36. (p. 106)

In this example, Leah demonstrates her ability to structure the whole space by mentally coordinating the one row and one column that she has constructed with the tiles and iterating that row. Her complete mental structuring of the space as an array of six groups of six lets her then use multiplication to determine the total count of units.

Research by Outhred and Mitchelmore (2000) not only confirms the developmental progression just described, but also demonstrates that drawing can indicate a child's level of two-dimensional spatial structuring. Outhred and Mitchelmore presented tasks to children in grades 1–4, asking them to determine how many of a given unit square would be needed to cover a particular rectangular region. In one task, the dimensions of the unit and the rectangular region were given and drawn on paper, but manipulative materials such as tiles were not provided. Instead, the children primarily used drawing strategies to solve the rectangle-covering tasks, and some used rulers to support their drawing work. A close look at the drawings they produced reveal different developmental levels of spatial structuring. Early levels are marked by drawings with incomplete or unsystematic coverings. When children first show a completed covering, they use individually drawn units. Later levels find children covering an area using some row (or column) iteration and even measurement of one dimension using the units. Finally, children rely less on drawing and are able to calculate counts of units using the size of the unit, the dimensions of the rectangular region, and multiplication or repeated addition. These levels—identified and described in Outhred and Mitchelmore's research through the children's drawings— indicate the gradual development of children's abilities to structure and represent the space of a rectangular region, leading toward their recognition of the multiplicative structure of a rectangular array.

In case 19, Georgia asks her students to draw a 3 by 4 array, and the drawings her students produce (see Figure 36) are consistent with both Battista's study and Outhred and Mitchelmore's research.

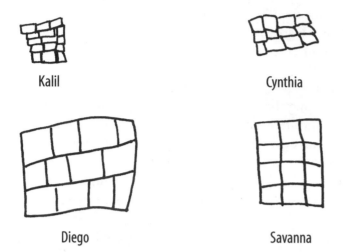

Figure 36 Four ways of drawing a 3 by 4 array.

When first asked to draw the 3 by 4 array, Kalil, who has a tentative hold on an array's structure, draws the units one at a time. Even more interesting to note—and more indicative of Kalil's level of spatial structuring at the beginning of the case—is Georgia's description of his drawing process. According to Georgia, when Kalil draws his units, he begins with a row across the top. He then draws units in a column down the right side, but without counting the corner in common. When he fills in the units within this "frame," he gets an extra row. Cynthia also draws the squares one at a time, but her drawing does result in an accurate count of the units. Diego's drawing reveals that he has begun to recognize and construct some understanding of the array structure, but he does not yet coordinate the rows and columns. He draws rows when asked to draw the 3 by 4 array, but his squares are not aligned in columns. Savanna demonstrates row and column coordination in her drawing. She draws full-length horizontal and vertical lines through a rectangle to indicate the composite units—the rows and columns—that make up the array. As was the case in Outhred and Mitchelmore's research, the children's drawings and their drawing process offer Georgia valuable insights into their spatial structuring.

The research of Outhred and Mitchelmore (2000), the research of Battista et al. (1998), and Georgia's case differ in the tasks given to the children and the medium used to solve the spatial structuring tasks.

However, these studies and the casebook examples all point to the significance of the row (and column) as a repeated unit in the child's structuring of two-dimensional space.

Three-dimensional space presents similar spatial structuring challenges, because children must come to see the series of layers that constitute volume measures. Research by Battista and Clements (Battista, 1998; Battista & Clements, 1996, 1998) describes the strategies students may employ as they count the cubes in rectangular cube buildings; the reasoning involved in this work sets the foundation for the child's understanding of volume. According to this research, children at one level of spatial structuring demonstrate no organization in their counting of the cubes. At another level, students may count every face showing on a cube because they cannot yet coordinate the different views of the building and do not recognize that a top face and a side face may be shared by one cube. With this strategy, children's volume measures remain inaccurate because they count some cubes twice, some three times, and some (those in the interior which they cannot see) not at all. Derek, a third grader in Lydia's classroom (case 27), demonstrates a level in which what is not seen is not counted. Faced with the task of counting the color cubes in a clear, three-dimensional rectangular container, Derek counts the faces of the cubes he sees on the top and the four sides of the container in an organized manner, but he forgets that cubes also go down the middle of the solid. At the most sophisticated level of structuring in three-dimensional space, children not only are able to visualize the interior units, but also come to use a layering strategy. Efren articulates such a strategy when counting cubes in Rita Lucia's case 28:

> "I counted the bottom and there were 24 squares. That is kind of a layer on the bottom. Then I saw that the sides were all three high. So then I thought, I need two more layers of 24 squares to fill up the box. It is 72." (p. 159)

Children's recognition of three-dimensional space as a series of layers allows them to count the number of units in one layer and then multiply or skip count to arrive at the total count of cubic units (Battista, 1998, Battista & Clements, 1996, 1998; Lehrer, in press). In this way, the structure of three-dimensional space, like that of two-dimensional space, leads children to apply multiplicative reasoning.

As is evident from the research and from the episodes reported in this casebook, spatial structuring is a demanding task; it requires considerable time for children to fully develop this mental ability. From a developmental perspective, spatial structuring is challenging because it requires that the child focus on and coordinate more than one aspect or dimension of an object at a time. Once children have that ability, they can then better coordinate the origin and endpoint in linear measure and the rows and columns in a rectangular array. Their ability to coordinate rows and columns in two dimensions will then support their work in measuring the volume of three-dimensional solids. Over time, children develop an increasing ability to take multiple perspectives. The ability to coordinate the multiple views (front view, side view, top view) of a three-dimensional structure lessens the likelihood of double-counting some faces or missing the interior cubes and thus is critical to the child's measurement of volume (Battista & Clements, 1998).

This discussion would not be complete without noting that spatial structuring, though a mental organization and construct, is based on action. Throughout the casebook, we see children building arrays with square tiles, filling containers with cubes and acorns, pointing as they count individual tiles or cubes, and using sweeping gestures with their hands across rows, columns, and layers, whether built with manipulatives or drawn on paper. These actions are not just motor actions; they are mental actions as well. The sequences of motion—the building, filling, drawing, and counting motions—described throughout the casebook are the coordinating actions that children look at and reflect upon in order to further organize their spatial structuring (Battista & Clements, 1996; Battista et al., 1998). Whatever the medium for action and reflection—concrete materials or drawings—it falls to the child to establish the structural relationships in a set of objects. Spatial structuring is not itself a property in an array or cube building. It is a "putting into relation"—a coordination and integration—that each individual must construct (Battista et al., 1998; Battista & Clements, 1996; Piaget & Inhelder, 1967).

Tools of measurement

As children develop their abilities to use the measuring tools available in the world around them, they must confront a variety of issues if they are to use these tools with understanding and meaning, not merely with rote procedures or techniques.

Measuring tools conveniently iterate and number units of measure, making the measurement process easier and much more efficient. We use rulers and tape measures as tools for linear measure, measuring cups for volume, and grids of squares (although not numbered) as "rulers" for area. These measuring tools are part of our culture, and children encounter them every day in practical measurement (Schliemann, Carraher, & Ceci, 1997). From these informal experiences, children begin to form notions about the use of measuring devices, just as Barbara's kindergartners (in case 2) articulate their awareness of and prior home experiences with a tape measure:

> TEACHER: What's a measuring tape?
>
> TAMMY: What you measure stuff with.
>
> TEACHER: You measure stuff with a measuring tape. But what is it?
>
> TAMMY: It's a tool that measures things so you know if it is big or small.
>
> ELLEN: I have one at home. My dad used it to measure me. (pp. 11–12)

Bragg's research (Bragg & Outhred, 2000) emphasizes the need to pay attention to the child's conceptual understanding to ensure meaningful use of a measuring tool. In Bragg's study, the majority of students between grade 1 and grade 5 improved in their measurement techniques using nonstandard units and rulers, but over these years their conceptual understandings of unit and unit iteration did not show the same growth. Even in grade 5, some students were unsuccessful in measurement tasks

515

520

525

530

that required knowledge of what constitutes a unit and an understanding of how rulers are constructed; in one task, they were unsuccessful when asked to measure a line using a "broken" ruler (scale marked from 4 to 20 centimeters). Bragg attributes the lack of conceptual growth to the fact that many classroom measurement experiences are reduced to rote procedures with measuring tools. The students become proficient in lining up one end of the ruler against one end of an object and simply reading the number on the ruler at the other end of the object, but they do not come to a conceptual understanding of the relationships between the units, unit iteration, and the measurement scale of the tool.

Historically, body parts—handspans, feet, arm lengths—were the first tools of measurement, and they continue to be the basis of measurement systems in some cultures today (Schliemann, Carraher, & Ceci, 1997). By using nonstandard body units of measure as a basis for comparing two objects, children can build a foundation for the meaningful use of conventional measurement devices. Children's own construction of tools can also foster their understanding of not only the conventional units but also the process of measuring with a tool (Van de Walle, 1998).

As students choose a measuring tool, they must consider which aspect of an object they are measuring, and whether it is a measure of one, two, or three dimensions, in order to select a tool with appropriate units. In the discussion of unit (section 3 of this essay), we noted that some of Lydia's students (case 21) try to use a ruler—a tool for linear measure—to measure the area of their hands. We also see children's confusion as Janine's students (case 18) lay out square tiles to measure the perimeter of a rectangle. In these cases, students are still learning to understand the dimensions they are measuring and to identify the most appropriate tool for that measurement.

The majority of research on measurement devices focuses on the child's use of the ruler. This research, however, presents conflicting views. Some researchers insist that for meaningful use of rulers, children must first be able to conserve length, make indirect comparisons, and understand the part-whole relationship between the total length and the smaller units of the whole (Kamii & Clark, 1997). Other researchers in the field disagree with such "prerequisites" for ruler use, particularly when children are engaged in meaningful problem solving. Here we can again call upon the study (cited in section 3 of this essay) in which conventional rulers were not problematic for six- to eight-year-olds as they compared and communicated over the telephone the length of line segments drawn

535

540

545

550

555

560

565

570

on a piece of paper (Nunes, Light, & Mason, 1993). It may be that, as Clements (1999) suggests, rulers are cultural tools that children can learn to use before they develop the "prerequisite" abilities that other researchers propose. Children can then use their ruler skills in authentic measurement experiences that further develop their understanding of measurement concepts.

As noted in the discussion of nonstandard and standard units in this essay, this latter position on children's ruler use, although still exploratory in nature, questions the instructional practices that typically begin with nonstandard units and move to the eventual use of standard units and conventional measurement tools. Activities using student-constructed measurement devices and nonstandard units are still essential, but a more fluid approach to tool use is being suggested in the research, with an emphasis on the meaningful use of such conventional tools as rulers. Teachers must be aware, however, that a child's correct reading of a ruler does not always reflect a true understanding of fundamental measurement concepts.

Though debate may persist over the prerequisites for ruler use, we do have consistent documentation of the issues that arise when children work with rulers. The most important concept for children to recognize is that each unit on the ruler is a linear distance, not a location on the tool. When shown a ruler and asked, "Would you show me one inch?" a child who does not yet see the marked interval of linear distance as the unit will simply point to the number 1 or to the line at that single point (Kamii, 1995). Children also have difficulty because they tend to focus on the position of only one endpoint when measuring length, rather than on the distance between the beginning and ending points (Clements & Battista, 1986; Hiebert, 1984). For instance, many third, fourth, and fifth graders will read 5 cm as the length of the line below when in fact the line is only 3 cm long. (This is similar to the "broken ruler" task reported in the research of Bragg, described earlier in this section.)

Few young children understand that any point on a ruler can be used as the starting point. Children also demonstrate confusion about the zero point and edge of the ruler. Josie (case 16) writes of a student who has difficulty with the starting point of the tool:

One boy did not start his measurement at the end of the tape measure; it had a small metal tab at the end, and the student ignored this part and started his measurement after the tab. (In fact, he folded the tab back to get it out of the way.) (p. 81)

Other students in Josie's case articulate their understanding of an implied zero on the ruler, as well as the notion that they must count the linear distance between the numbers on the ruler:

MARCUS: They didn't put it there, but at the end of the ruler there is a zero.

TEACHER: [*pointing to the end with the 12*] At the end? Way down here?

MARCUS: No, the other end, the beginning.

TEACHER: So the end with the 1 is the beginning. Then why did Robby say we start with the zero? I still don't see a zero.

DEB: Because when you start at 1 on a tape measure or something, you should already have one inch.

RAUL: [*yelling out*] It's zero inches! You have to start at zero because that is where the inches start!

ROBBY: Yeah, the number 1 is at the end of one inch, not at the beginning. (p. 82)

Gradually, through many experiences with measuring tools in practical, meaningful activities, children refine their understandings and learn to differentiate among tools. As a result, they become more discriminating in their tool selection. In Mary's case 1, Jenny suggests using a tape measure to measure the perimeter of a puddle and reasons, "I would use a tape measure because it bends" (p. 7). This thinking illustrates one child's growing ability to discriminate among tools and select one that will best serve her purpose. The second graders in Mabel's case 15 mention the "lines between the lines" on rulers, illustrating an awareness (but not yet an understanding) of the structure and calibration of rulers that can yield greater precision in measurement. Through extended experience with a variety of measuring tools, children begin to see that tools vary in their ease of use, efficiency, and accuracy (Schwartz, 1995).

Figuring out formulas

An understanding of unit, spatial structuring, and the decomposing and recomposing of space lay the foundation for understanding formulas. Students can then make connections among formulas and apply them meaningfully.

Formulas can serve as shortcuts for efficiently determining a measure. In Sandra's case 24, Wallace proclaims his own formula for determining the area of the isosceles trapezoids the class has been investigating:

> "Take the base and add the top. Take that answer and multiply by the height, and then take half." (p. 132)

Here, Wallace has described the standard formula for the area of a trapezoid, conventionally represented as $\frac{1}{2}h\,(b_1 + b_2)$. Geoboard activities, group discussions, and the sharing of trapezoid examples in his classroom led Wallace to his own expression of the formula.

What concepts must students develop in order to understand formulas and apply them with meaning? Consider the formula for the area of a rectangle, area = length × width ($A = l \times w$). Covering a rectangular region with unit squares helps children understand area measure, but the formula itself formally connects area, linear measurements, and multiplication (Outhred & Mitchelmore, 2000). Both Outhred and Mitchelmore (2000) and Simon and Blume (1994) assert that in order to understand these connections, students must be able to structure the space into a rectangular array of squares, a structure in which each row or column has the same number of square units. Moreover, children must recognize the relationship between the unit of area and the unit used to measure the length of the sides, and that the number of area units in each row or column and the number of rows or columns in the array can be determined from the lengths of the sides of the rectangle. Thus, the count of area units is determined by multiplying the count of the linear units of the rectangle's length and width.

In the case of a rectangle measuring 6 inches by 5 inches, students must first mentally recognize the array of six rows and five columns that

645

650

655

660

665

forms the space. What's more, they must recognize that each unit counted to determine the area is a square measuring 1 inch by 1 inch. Traditional classroom instruction often just gives students the area units to be used in a problem, but recognizing the relationship between an area unit and its linear dimensions is critical if students are to understand both the area formula and the meaning of the square units (Simon & Blume, 1994). Though most of the research about arrays and the area formula presupposes square units, other units are possible, and, depending on the situation, some area units may appear more convenient than others. For example, triangular units can seem more useful in some situations. When students begin to develop formulas, however, the value of square units becomes apparent. Square units make possible the straightforward counting and multiplication entailed in area formulas.

Just as the area formula for rectangles builds from concepts of spatial structuring, so too does the formula for the volume of a rectangular solid, volume = length × width × height ($V = l \times w \times h$). In order to apply this formula with understanding, students must understand the connection between the linear measurements and the volume of the three-dimensional space, which means they must be able to mentally structure the three-dimensional space into layers. They must also recognize how the linear measurements define the units of volume. Research conducted by Heaton (1992) describes one group of fifth graders who measured the length of a sandbox to be 46 yards, the width to be 10 yards, and the height to be 1 foot. The teacher then instructed the students to multiply $46 \times 10 \times 1$ to find the volume. Here, both students and teacher misapplied what was for them a rote procedure. The product of these linear measurements did not reflect a standard cubic unit of volume—neither a cubic yard nor a cubic foot. Of course, as in the case of area measurement, other units are possible, but by defining units and making connections to the volume formula, students can discover the value of the conventional cubic unit.

Work with measurement formulas can provide geometric models that help students understand the properties of multiplication. As students become increasingly fluent with the multiplicative structure of arrays and the area formula, they see in action the commutative property of multiplication: an array of six rows, five units each, has an area of 6×5, or 30, as does the 5×6 array made from five rows, six units each. Similarly, as students learn to structure three-dimensional space into layers and connect this structure to the $V = l \times w \times h$ formula for volume, they see firsthand the associative property of multiplication; for example, $(3 \times 4) \times 5 = 3 \times (4 \times 5)$.

Connections can be made among many measurement formulas, and when students have the chance to uncover these connections, they are less likely to view these formulas as merely a list of isolated rules to memorize (Van de Walle, 1998). The decomposing and recomposing of space discussed in section 2 of this essay can illuminate the connections among the area formulas for parallelograms, triangles, and trapezoids. For example, by decomposing and recomposing space, a parallelogram can be transformed into a rectangle that has the same base and height measurements as the original parallelogram.

The area formula for a rectangle can then be used to determine the area of the transformed parallelogram. This implies the generalized area formula of area = base × height ($A = b \times h$) for any parallelogram (Van de Walle, 1998). (A slightly more elaborate argument must be used to prove that the formula holds for all parallelograms.)

In Rachel's case 23, third and fourth graders use the area measurement of a 4 cm by 5 cm rectangle to determine the area of a right triangle and an isosceles triangle drawn inside the rectangle.

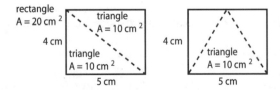

They reason that the area of the triangle is one-half that of the rectangle, or 10 square centimeters. Noah explains this:

> "You find the area of the rectangle. Then since you have split the rectangle in half [with the triangle], you just divide its area by 2." (p. 128)

Rachel's students then tackle the problem of determining the area of a scalene triangle within the rectangle. While they are not yet using formulas, they are well on their way to uncovering and proving that the area of any triangle is one-half the area of a rectangle with the same base and height. Their recognition of the connections between rectangles and triangles is a step toward understanding the general area formula for a triangle, $A = \frac{1}{2}b \times h$.

Another example appears in Sandra's case 24. When attempting to determine the area of a trapezoid, the seventh grader Ashraf announces a decomposing and recomposing strategy. Ashraf explains:

> "I split the trapezoid into a rectangle and triangles. I found the area of each piece, and then added them all together." (p. 131)

Indra, a classmate, then integrates this decomposing and recomposing of space with the linear measurements of the trapezoid:

> "It's actually a rule that uses numbers for the trapezoid to find the area. [She pauses.] First take the base and subtract the top. Take that answer and multiply it by the height, and then cut it in half. That answer is the area of the triangles all together. Then take the top times the height, and that is the area of the rectangle. Add the two answers together and you get the area." (p. 132)

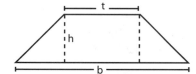 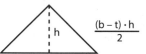 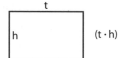

The trapezoid formula that Indra suggests can be expressed as

$$\frac{(b_1 - b_2)h}{2} + b_2h$$

This formula is equivalent to Wallace's trapezoid formula mentioned earlier in this theme, which can be expressed as $\frac{1}{2}h(b_1 + b_2)$. Indra's approach is based on her decomposing and recomposing of space, while Wallace's formula is based on his analysis of the numbers from several trapezoid examples in the classroom (though it could also be based on decomposing space). These classmates arrive at two different approaches that lead to different but equivalent formulas.

The examples cited above demonstrate connections among area formulas; similar connections exist among volume formulas. For a rectangular prism, the volume formula, $V = l \times w \times h$, can be restated as $V = (\text{area of the base}) \times h$. In that formula, the area of the base indicates

Measuring Space in One, Two, and Three Dimensions

the number of cubes in each layer of the prism (calling to mind spatial structuring); the squares in the area of the base are actually the bottom faces of the cubes in the first layer. The height used in the formula indicates how many of these layers of cubes you have. Students who do not understand how the formula maps onto the prism may simply multiply the area of the base by the area of a vertical face, a common student misconception reported by W. G. Martin (personal communication, August 18, 2000). With some elaboration that the reader may wish to pursue, the formula $V = $ (area of the base) $\times h$ can be extended to a variety of prisms and cylinders. It can be shown that regardless of the shape of the base, the volume still equals the area of the base times the height.

S E C T I O N **7**

Different measures, different relationships

Relationships between specific measures of space are not always obvious or straightforward. The relationships between area and perimeter and those between surface area and volume are especially complex because as a shape changes, the relationships between these measures may change in a variety of ways. This renders these relationships elusive to children—and adults!

As difficult as it is for some children to differentiate area (a two-dimensional measure) from perimeter (a linear measure), it is perhaps even more challenging for them to determine how these two measures change in relation to one another as the shape changes. The difficulty is that there is no single way to characterize the changes. Two two-dimensional shapes can have the same area, but different perimeters; they can have different areas but the same perimeter; or one can have a larger area and a smaller perimeter (see Figures 37–39). The area of a shape can change while its perimeter remains the same, and the perimeter of a shape can be altered while its area remains the same.

In Suzanne's case 30, third graders explore these relationships between area and perimeter as they compare these measurements for different

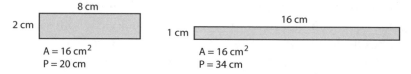

A = 16 cm²   A = 16 cm²
P = 20 cm   P = 34 cm

Figure 37 Two rectangles with equal area and different perimeters.

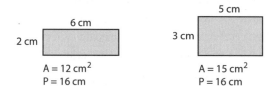

A = 12 cm²   A = 15 cm²
P = 16 cm   P = 16 cm

Figure 38 Two rectangles with equal perimeters but different areas.

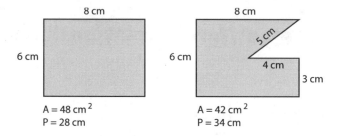

A = 48 cm²   A = 42 cm²
P = 28 cm   P = 34 cm

Figure 39 The shape with the larger area has the smaller perimeter.

rectangles. We can hear Vic's surprise at finding that the rectangles could have different perimeters but the same area:

> "Ours has a perimeter of 30 and an area of 36, but this other one has a perimeter of 40 and still an area of 36. And look at this one. It has a perimeter of 24 and an area of 36. How can that be?"

Bridget, a classmate, responds:

> "That's ours . . . It's right. See, it's a square. The perimeter is all sixes, so that's 6 + 6 = 12 and 12 + 12 = 24, so it's right. And the area is 36. We counted the tiles. It's right." (p. 170)

Bridget's work points to the fact that, of all four-sided shapes, the square has the largest area for a given perimeter. (If all shapes are considered—not only those with straight sides—the circle has the largest area; it "pushes" the given perimeter out as far as possible in all directions to enclose the greatest amount of space.)

The relationship between surface area and volume is also complex. While volume refers to the amount of space contained within a three-dimensional shape, surface area refers to the amount of area that covers that shape on all sides. Changing the volume may or may not change the surface area of a solid, and two solids with the same volume can have different surface areas (see Figure 40).

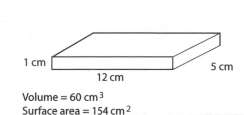

3 cm
4 cm
5 cm
Volume = 60 cm^3
Surface area = 94 cm^2

1 cm
12 cm
5 cm
Volume = 60 cm^3
Surface area = 154 cm^2

Figure 40 Two solids with equal volume but different surface areas.

Companies concerned with the cost and amount of packaging material may give careful attention to the relationship between surface area and volume for a given shape; they may want to package their product in a box with dimensions that yield the least surface area for a given volume. Of all rectangular solids, the cube has the largest volume for a given surface area. (If all solids are considered, the sphere has the largest volume for a given surface area.)

Consider how the surface area and volume change when we link interlocking cubes; this process demonstrates why the relationship between the two measures may be so elusive to children. When we link two cubes, the volume doubles from one cubic unit to two cubic units, but the surface area—the faces showing—is not simply double that of one cube. Two of the faces are now connected and are no longer showing, so we cannot count them as surface area. In Lucy's case 32, third graders are coming to grips with this very idea as they debate the surface area of a two-cube tower by counting the faces of the cubes:

MOIRA: You're not supposed to count this part. [*She pulls apart the two cubes and points to the top and bottom attached faces.*] So that's not a side when they're together. That would be 10.

SARAH: Yeah, 10…. But there are two cubes, so that means there would have to be 12. [*She is remembering that one cube has 6 square units.*]

TEACHER:	Sarah says that because there are two cubes and one cube has 6, then two cubes must be 12.
MOIRA:	But this part is stuck together, so this part doesn't count. [*She pulls the cubes apart and points to the two hidden square units.*]
SARAH:	Oh, so the bottom of this and the top of this don't count.
JEFF:	The top one of this [bottom cube] and the bottom one of this [top cube] don't count. (p. 175)

Lucy notes that throughout this work, the children are continually pointing to the faces of the cubes as they count, rotating and flipping the cube tower, pulling the cubes apart, and counting faces again. Children's construction of measurement concepts is grounded in their actions, in concrete experiences, and in the physical manipulation of space.

Eventually, Lucy's students use a chart to record the number of cubes and the corresponding surface area of each larger tower they make. From this chart, they recognize a pattern in the sequence of surface area measurements for a single-cube tower that grows by one cube each time: "Every time you add a cube, you add on a surface area of 4" (p. 178). Although the rule that Lucy's students articulate is specific to their cube towers, finding this relationship does allow them to see some order in their surface area and volume work.

Although this discussion has focused on young children's efforts to make sense of the relationships between different measures of space, these relationships can be an issue for older children and many adults as well. A study by Woodward and Byrd (1983) presented eighth graders and college students with a series of different rectangles ("gardens"), each with a different area but all with the same perimeter; the task was to determine which rectangle was the "biggest." Almost two-thirds of the participants in the study responded that all the rectangles were the same size; they failed to differentiate between area and perimeter and seemed to lack an understanding that regions of the same perimeter could differ in area. Another study found that college students relied blindly on formulas, not conceptual understanding, to solve problems involving surface area and volume (Enochs & Gabel, 1984). This research suggests the need to support both preservice and in-service teachers in further developing their own understanding of these measurement concepts. If we as teachers are going to help children develop their mathematical ideas, then we need to develop our own mathematical ideas as well.

While such research provides evidence that older children and adults encounter difficulties in understanding the relationships between different measures of space, very little research explores how younger children address this issue. In this section of the research essay, the discussion of elementary children's efforts relies entirely on the episodes described in this casebook. The teachers writing these cases, then, have added to and extended the limited research in the field. This points to the importance of continuing conversations between teachers and researchers. Research is not a static, fixed body of facts in mathematics education. Rather, research is dynamic in nature, and mathematics education is in a constant state of revision, evolution, and change, based in part on observations of the young mathematicians who are at work in our classrooms.

CONCLUSION

The research and the cases we have presented call attention to the need for meaningful mathematical experiences in the classroom. Children must not merely follow rote measurement procedures, but build an understanding of the measurement process in all dimensions of space. With these experiences and with effective questioning from a reflective teacher, children construct their own "big ideas" of measurement, and these "big ideas" become the subject of conversations shared by all learners in the classroom. Some of our children will have the same ideas as those we see in the cases and in the research discussed in this essay; some of our children will have much different ideas. The power comes in opening our eyes, our ears, and our minds to the mathematical ideas of our own students. As we watch, listen, and question, we, too, can become active researchers in the classroom.

REFERENCES

Battista, M. (1998). How many blocks? *Mathematics Teaching in the Middle School, 3*(6), 404–411.

Battista, M. (1999). The importance of spatial structuring in geometric reasoning. *Teaching Children Mathematics, 6*(3), 170–177.

Battista, M. & Clements, D. (1996). Students' understanding of three-dimensional rectangular arrays of cubes. *Journal for Research in Mathematics Education, 27*(3), 258–292.

Battista, M. & Clements, D. (1998). Finding the number of cubes in rectangular cube buildings. *Teaching Children Mathematics, 4*(5), 258–264.

Battista, M., Clements, D., Arnoff, J., Battista, K., & Burrow, C. V. A. (1998). Students' spatial structuring of 2-D arrays of squares. *Journal of Research in Mathematics Education, 29*, 503–532.

Bishop, A. (1983). Space and geometry. In R. Lesh & M. Lander (Eds.), *Acquisition of mathematics concepts and processes* (pp. 175–203). New York: Academic Press.

Bragg, P. & Outhred, L. (2000). What is taught versus what is learnt: The case of linear measurement. In J. Bana & A. Chapman (Eds.), *Mathematics education beyond 2000: Proceedings of the 23rd annual conference of the Mathematics Education Research Group of Australasia* (pp. 112–118). Perth: MERGA.

Carpenter, T. P. (1976). Analysis and synthesis of existing research on measurement. In R. Lesh & D. Bradbard (Eds.), *Number and measurement: Papers from a research workshop*, ERIC. (ERIC Document Reproduction Service No. ED 120 027).

Clements, D. (1999). Teaching length measurement: Research challenges. *School Science and Mathematics, 99*(1), 5–11.

Clements, D. H. & Battista, M. T. (1986). Geometry and geometric measurement. *Arithmetic Teacher, 33*(6), 29–32.

Clements, D. H. & Battista, M. T. (2001). Length, perimeter, area, and volume. In L. S. Grinstein & S. I. Lipsey (Eds.), *Encyclopedia of mathematics.* New York: Routledge Falmer.

Copeland, R. W. (1984). *How children learn mathematics: Teaching implications of Piaget's research* (4th ed.). New York: Macmillan.

Enochs, L. G. & Gabel, D. L. (1984). Preservice elementary teachers' conceptions of volume. *School Science and Mathematics, 84*(8), 670–680.

Heaton, R. (1992). Who is minding the mathematics content? A case study of a fifth-grade teacher. *Elementary School Journal, 93*(2), 153–162.

Hiebert, J. (1981). Cognitive development and learning linear measurement. *Journal for Research in Mathematics Education, 12*, 197–211.

Hiebert, J. (1984). Why do some children have trouble learning measurement concepts? *Arithmetic Teacher, 31*(7), 19–24.

Kamii, C. (1995, October). *Why is the use of a ruler so hard?* Paper presented at the Seventeenth Annual Meeting of the North American Chapter of the International Group for the Psychology of Mathematics Education, Columbus, Ohio.

Kamii, C. & Clark, F. B. (1997). Measurement of length: The need for a better approach to teaching. *School Science and Mathematics, 97*(3), 116–121.

Lehrer, R. (in press). Developing understanding of measurement. In J. Kilpatrick, W. G. Martin, & D. Schifter (Eds.), *A research companion to the Principles and Standards for School Mathematics.* Reston, VA: National Council of Teachers of Mathematics.

Lehrer, R., Jenkins, M., & Osana, H. (1998). Longitudinal study of children's reasoning about space and geometry. In R. Lehrer & D. Chazan (Eds.), *Designing learning environments for developing understanding of geometry and space* (pp. 137–167). Mahwah, NJ: Lawrence Erlbaum.

McClain, K., Cobb, P., Gravemeijer, K., & Estes, B. (1999). Developing mathematical reasoning within the context of measurement. In L. Stiff & F. Curcio (Eds.), *Developing mathematical reasoning in grades K–12* (pp. 93–106). Reston, VA: National Council of Teachers of Mathematics.

Nitabach, E. & Lehrer, R. (1996). Developing spatial sense through area measurement. *Teaching Children Mathematics, 2,* 473–476.

Nunes, T., Light, P., & Mason, J. H. (1993). Tools for thought: The measurement of length and area. *Learning and Instruction, 3,* 39–54.

Outhred, L. & McPhail, D. (2000). A framework for teaching early measurement. In J. Bana & A. Chapman (Eds.), *Mathematics education beyond 2000: Proceedings of the 23rd annual conference of the Mathematics Education Research Group of Australasia* (pp. 487–494). Perth: MERGA.

Outhred, L. & Mitchelmore, M. (2000). Young children's intuitive understanding of rectangular area measurement. *Journal for Research in Mathematics Education, 31*(2), 144–167.

Paley, V. G. (1981). Wally's stories. Cambridge, MA: Harvard University Press.

Piaget, J. & Inhelder, B. (1967). *The child's conception of space.* New York: W. W. Norton.

Reynolds, A. & Wheatley, G. H. (1996) Elementary students' construction and coordination of units in an area setting. *Journal for Research in Mathematics Education, 27*(5), 564–581.

Rowan, T. & Lindquist, M. (1989). The measurement standards. *Arithmetic Teacher, 37*(2), 22–6.

Schliemann, A. D., Carraher, D. W., & Ceci, S. J. (1997). Everyday cognition. In J. W. Berry, P. R. Dasen, T. S. Saraswathi (Eds.), *Handbook of cross-cultural psychology* (2nd ed.) (pp. 177–216). Boston, MA: Allyn and Bacon.

Schwartz, S. (1995). Developing power in linear measurement. *Teaching Children Mathematics, 1*(7), 412–416.

Simon, M. A. & Blume, G. W. (1994). Building and understanding multiplicative relationships. *Journal for Research in Mathematics Education, 25*(5), 472–494.

Thompson, C. S. & Van de Walle, J. (1985). Learning about rulers and measuring. *Arithmetic Teacher, 32*(8), 8–12.

Van de Walle, J. A. (1998). Elementary and middle school mathematics: *Teaching developmentally* (3rd ed.). New York: Longman.

Wilson, P. S. & Rowland, R. (1993). Teaching measurement. In R. Jensen (Ed.), *Research ideas for the classroom: Early childhood mathematics* (pp. 171–194). New York: Macmillan.

Woodward, E. & Byrd, F. (1983). Area: Included topic, neglected concept. *School Science and Mathematics, 83*(4), 343–347.